ISRAEL
INSIDE
OUT

Herbert Geduld

Israel Inside Out

Abelard-Schuman
London New York Toronto

Library of Congress Catalogue Card Number: 77-75456
Standard Book Number: 200.71621.2
First Printed in the United States of America in 1970
First Published in Great Britain in 1970

LONDON	NEW YORK	TORONTO
Abelard-Schuman	Abelard-Schuman	Abelard-Schuman
Limited	Limited	Canada Limited
8 King St. WC2	257 Park Ave. So.	1680 Midland Ave.

An Intext Publisher

Printed in the United States of America

TO TOBY
without whom,
living in Israel,
or anywhere,
would be impossible

CONTENTS

Introduction II

I

Who Put That Great Big Hippo in
Those Ten-Thousand Iddy Biddy Cans?

II

Vitamin P

III

Wanted: A Good Geves Man

IV

Kolboinik

V

Bar Mitzvah Country Style

INTRODUCTION

Every year tens of thousands of American Jewish tourists descend upon Israel, oh and ah over the Jewish policemen and the Jewish porters, photograph their way through forests of film, soak in the sun and sand, and return to America tanned and thrilled at the phenomenon called Israel.

A few, a very few, remain here or plan to come back here. My wife and I are two that did. This book is our reaction to our five years in the country. There are tons of travel guides and tourist books on Israel. This is not one of them. This is a book about rain and water, about radios, flies, lizards and storks, about parking and prostitutes, about building blocks and bowling greens; in short, it is a kaleidoscope of the impressions a young Midwestern American couple get from this fascinating land.

I suppose if an American wants to adjust to Israel easier (no one, no one, can adjust to Israel easily), he should live in Arizona first, where climate, flora and fauna, are somewhat similar. We didn't. We lived in Cleveland and Detroit, and then moved to Israel from the 38° below zero winter of St. James, Minnesota; so our impressions are stronger than most.

The only thing that is constant in Israel is change and since most of this book was written before the Six Day War, two or three of the incidents are now historical and one strangely prophetic; they have been left unchanged for that reason.

This is not a book about fighting in Israel, it is a book about living in Israel.

This is a book of facts and quite a bit of fancy. If the reader gets the impression that much of it is written with tongue-in-cheek, he is correct.

It is a book tinged, we hope, with laughter — and we know tinged with love.

I

Who Put That
Great Big Hippo
in Those
Ten-Thousand
Iddy Biddy Cans?

UNDERCOVER IN ISRAEL

There comes a day in every new immigrant's life when he feels that at long last he is a part of Israel, he really belongs. This day came for me not when I bought my home here, not when I became a new immigrant officially, but by a much closer to home occurrence, the day I put on my first pair of Israeli underwear.

If you're a typical American settler, you come here with seven years of changes of kids' clothes and maybe a few spare things for yourself, but sooner or later the day dawns when your last pair of underwear gives up manfully after months of battling Israeli detergents, and disintegrates in your hands.

Your wife, thoughtful creature that she is, has anticipated this day and solemnly presents you with an introduction to the Israeli textile industry, your first pair of genuinely Israeli-designed and Israeli-produced underwear. One thing in Israel is certain: the size you wore in America has no relation to the size you wear in Israel. In fact, the sizes on one brand of clothes in a store on the right side of Herzel Street usually have little relationship to the size on similar clothes by another manufacturer in a store on the opposite side of the street.

Needless to say, the undershirt I unpacked was designed to fit an undernourished Eucalyptus tree and although it made it over my head, it could not make it over my shoulders. We take it back, of course, and since I'm a small guy we buy the largest undershirt available. It makes it over the shoulders alright, but it was obviously designed for a sunken-chested racer as the girdle-like grip around my chest testifies. This, however, one gets used to and after a few weeks of wear one manages to regain full use of his arms and lungs.

Shorts, well, shorts are a phenomenon all their own. The pair my wife bought me were either designed for a hermaphrodite or a guy with homosexual tendencies. Frankly about the closest things they resemble are a cross between a pair of my children's training pants and some old fashioned bloomers. They would serve marvelously as a costume for Baby Oncoming Year at a New Year's ball. One advantage, I think, they have, is that they come up to your armpits. Since the average Israeli has a tendency to sweat profusely in this hot climate, the added absorbtion is probably beneficial.

My first day as all Israeli underneath was not comfortable. My constricted chest was tugging against textile. My armpits were trying to get used to the proximity of elastic. But deep inside I had a warm glow. Now at last I was Israeli underside out.

SHAKY POLITICS

Any day now, I expect a clandestine visit from the secretariat of the Mapai party or at least from the prime minister's office. "Stop it," they will plead.

"It is wholly unheard of."

"A clever diabolic plot by the opposition parties to cause hysteria in the populace and bring about the downfall of the government."

"True, it is not legally punishable, but in the name of decency, desist, or it may create a greater effect on the stability of the country than devaluation."

What is this hideous unorthodox movement I am fostering? What is its modus operandi?

I stop for pedestrians.

Take this morning. I was turning into Shenkin Street from Achad Haam. A woman of about forty was in the carefully marked pedestrian crosswalk, and I was bearing down on her in typical Tel Aviv fashion, and then it happened. Right when I should have zoomed through the crosswalk missing her by inches (oops, excuse me, centimeters), I stopped and waved her on with my hand.

She froze to the spot thunderstruck. A clammy, cold sweat appeared on her body, her eyes gesticulated wildly, darting in every direction, pleading with passersby to help her out of this bizarre situation.

Slowly her earlier years of Haganah training (she looked Haganahish) came back to her. Struggling against an unprecedented situation, she plodded, as if in a trance, in front of my car to the other side of the street.

As I turned the corner, I could still see the look of incredulity on her face. Her faith in everything stable in Israel was shaken to the core.

Tomorrow morning I may stop for another pedestrian; that is, unless the Old Man drops in tonight. After all, you can't refuse a *landsman*.

PARKING LINGUISTICS

Let's face it squarely and state it emphatically. Hebrew is impossible to learn! Right? Right! Granted you'll find a certain percentage of people in Israel who speak it a certain percentage of the time. Granted the signs, cinema subtitles, newspapers, books, and radio jargon are in Hebrew, but still, for the average intelligent immigrant it is impossible to learn.

To begin with, it's written backwards. This, however, bothers no one except maybe Alan Lerner and Rex Harrison. But don't bring an English or American notebook to a Hebrew class. You've got to turn it inside out.

Second, don't be a lefty. If you are, don't immigrate. Once you're here, however, they do make some very nice special provisions. They've got lefty desks in the Hebrew University and the Technion.

Getting back to Hebrew, you don't learn it, you assimilate it. It seeps into you by some Semitic osmotic process and unless you determinedly fight this phenomenon, as a few German immigrants in the thirties did, you'll find suddenly that the gobbledygook on the radio makes sense.

The biggest surprise you get is when you start to read signs. This is sometimes, to tell the truth, not such a good surprise. To illustrate: for some weeks we found an excellent parking space in the heart of Tel Aviv. Of course there was a sign in Hebrew nearby, but since my Hebrew at the time was limited only to biblical phraseology, I couldn't make it out, or really never bothered trying for that matter.

However, I went to classes. Mind you, I didn't learn, I seeped. One day I seeped too far, a glance at the sign said: "Private Parking for Cars of the Swedish Consulate."

Now we had parked there for quite some time with no difficulty whatsoever. Of course, yumping yimming, our car happened to have Minnesota license plates, and of course, the ex-geography professor from Bratislava, who was probably the cop on duty, had a fingertip knowledge of the ethnic distribution of Swedes in America.

Anyway you figure it, we had parked freely, easily, with no qualms until we knew the language. Then our innate sense of decency, or better yet, fear of the short arm of the Israeli law, put a stop to this.

Last week, I parked for a while in a space reserved for the Philippine embassy.

Republic of the Philippines is quite a difficult thing to read in Hebrew.

DIGGING UP THE HOMESTEAD

I've got a friend over in Netanya who has somebody buried in his front yard. In fact, he has a small Byzantine tomb out near his kids' sandbox. He doesn't know exactly where now, because the tomb was filled in some years ago — the kids kept falling into it. That's the way it is with archeology in Israel. It's everywhere except where you're looking for it, or at least where I'm looking.

We've dug up our whole front and back yards, for grass actually, not for antiquities, but we hoped to find at least an old Roman shekel. No luck. We found barbed wire, broken glass, broken ceiling tiles, broken glass, rusty cans, broken glass — if anybody digs up our contemporary civilization, they'll surely believe we lived in glass houses.

When you build a home or a building in Israel, there is some kind of clause which specifies that if you should unearth any archeological items, they must be turned over to the local Department of Antiquities and the site must be examined by competent authorities before you are permitted to continue building. Most building contractors live in horror of ever discovering something on their land and losing time, money, and profits while it is excavated. The people that built my house had no such worries. We seem to have settled on one of the most virgin plots in Israel.

Some ex-kibbutznik buddies of mine tell me how, when they walked along their newly plowed fields after the first rains, they would come across fistfuls of ancient Roman and Hebrew coins. When I walk along the fields all I manage to pick up are thorns.

The mark of the amateur archeologist who has really made it in Israel is to have his lawn or patio strewn and littered with ancient Greek or Roman columns gathered from such places as Caesarea or Ashkelon. One of the homes in the neighboring town has quite a little coliseum going for him in his backyard. Of course, he's an old timer here and in pre-state days they probably figured if you're crazy enough to try to lift these granite paperweights, you deserve to take them home. Now the Israeli government frowns on the pilfering of its national treasures.

Archeology is the national pastime in Israel. The country, notwithstanding my dismal failures, just oozes artifacts. Mounds, tells, biblical sites, and prehistoric caves abound, awaiting the cash and catering of the would-be archeologist. There are some places where you just can't miss. For instance, Yigael Yadin, Israel's number one archeologist, is presently busy digging up Massada, a Herodian fortress and the place of the last Jewish stand against the Romans. He has made some phenomenal finds, but he's pitching with a big league team. Me, I'm going back to my kids' sandbox. There must be a tomb near it, somewhere.

AN ARMY MOVES ON ITS WHEELS

The first thing you notice about the Israeli Army is that it is everywhere. Everywhere. Buy a nice little ol' villa, (there are no houses in Israel, just apartments or villas) in the country away from it all, take a walk down one of the country lanes, and there, in all its camouflaged glory, is an army base. Take your family out for a drive along the sea, beautiful view, beautiful day; all of a sudden, boom, no road, just some gory skull and crossbones sign with Hebrew lettering, which you finally decipher to read "Rifle Range — No Entry."

Or try, if you're brave, insured, and mishuga, driving along the roads in Israel. If every third vehicle that passes you is not an army truck, tender, jeep, or command car, then there must be a war on somewhere. Since the Sinai campaign, I seriously believe the Israeli Army is constantly proving its vaunted maneuverability by seeing how fast and how often it can move itself from the northern Galilee to the southern Negev. I believe the Israeli soldier can be inducted, serve his two-year army duty and be discharged without ever getting off a moving vehicle.

It wouldn't be bad if only ordinary gigantic twenty-wheel trucks hurtled along the roads, but the colossal tank carriers are really frightening. Imagine yourself in a little Fiat putt-putting along at top speed of 35 miles an hour when along comes this multi-wheeled monster that passes and passes and passes and finally, thank goodness, passes you. Very few of the tank carriers ever carry tanks. This would dangerously effect their maneuverability.

As if tank carriers are not bad enough, there are also some hideous aberrations that carry planes which are tired of flying, and some enormous trucks that transport hush-hush things which nobody notices — right?

Once on the way home from work, we passed — yes, passed — an army truck. We immediately were gravely concerned. Was the truck stolen? Had the driver had a heart attack?

MICROWAVE MADNESS

On casual glance one gets the impression that time is a very precious thing in Israel. People are constantly running from place to place and impatience seems to be a national vice, or virtue. There is one organization, however, to which time means nothing, Kol Israel, "The Voice of Israel," the country's national radio broadcasting service.

Somehow in America you always associated radio broadcasts with punctuality. I remember that as a boy, I'd begin eating with Jack Armstrong and finish up by the Lone Ranger. In Israel if you turn on the radio to get your favorite program or to find out the approximate time, one out of three things usually happens.

One, you hear a beep, beep, beep sound, which means the station is between programs and can't think of anything better to say.

Two, you hear a small tune repeated over and over and over until it drives you crawling and frothing mad. This tune means the previous program ended early and the next one should start sometime, anytime. . . .

Three, you can't even find the damned station on the dial because its jumped to another frequency or gone off the air. Twenty-four hour radio service? Don't be ridiculous. A couple hours on this frequency, a couple hours on that, complete shutdown for coffee break. I don't know how many years one has to be in the country before he familiarizes himself with the vagaries of Israeli radio, but its certainly the mark of an old settler if he can flick the dial to his favorite program.

Even the radio newscasters don't seem to have grasped the ability to fill up or stretch out their allotted air time. In America it would seem incredible for an announcer whose program is scheduled to run until 9:30 to say . . .

"In thirteen seconds it will be a quarter-minute before 9:29," and then that ghastly tune repeating and repeating for the next minute.

One can only hope that this tendency does not carry on into Israeli television when it becomes available in the near future. If it does, the most prominent program on Israeli TV may be the test pattern.

THE HORA

One of the unfortunate things about America is that it does not have a national dance. Every dance America devises, and there have been many, is sooner or later internationalized. Take the twist, please. . . . Here is a dance(?) that is American in its inception and international (and perhaps immoral) in its performance.

Israel, however, does not have that problem. When Israel devised a national dance, the hora, it remained simply, purely, and forever Israeli. Nobody stole it, nobody adopted it, and frankly nobody, even in Israel, dances it. In the time we have been in Israel we have searched in vain for a good, honest, unrehearsed, spontaneous, joyful explosion of dance. We haven't found it.

Our hopes were aroused a few months ago when we received an announcement in the mail that proudly and bilingually exclaimed: "Dancing in the city square! Taught by professional native folk dance teacher!"

Dancing in the city square! *Tzenna! Tzenna!* Harry Belafonte! Here was our chance not only to see, but actually to dance, an honest-to-goodness Israeli hora.

In all fairness I must admit that I was not a party to the first lesson. My desire to partake in this phenomenon was overshadowed by my natural laziness and I fell asleep on the night of the first performance. My wife took the field for us. Along with our next door neighbor, she reported for duty at the city square promptly thirty minutes late.

I got the report the next morning. My wife danced for ninety solid minutes. She danced the polka, she danced the czardas, she danced the Norwegian national dance, she danced the Swiss national dance, she even danced some African dances to be attributed to some yet-to-emerge republics. The hora? Hora, shmora, who dances the hora in Israel?

WHO PUT THAT GREAT BIG HIPPO
IN THOSE TEN-THOUSAND IDDY BIDDY CANS?

I can't report this as the gospel truth because I'm too chicken to verify the facts, but the tale has so many fantastic potentialities that it is worth retelling.

It began about four or five years ago. There was a tremendous meat shortage in Israel. After years of meatless, vegetable-infested diets (statistic: Israel's per capita consumption of vegetables is the highest in the world), the Israeli public clamored for meat.

The scene shifts to Addis Abba. An Israeli road expert is trying to clear a road through the Ethiopian hinterland. Suddenly all building activity ceases. The swampy area the road must pass through is the happy hunting ground of hundreds of hippos.

Wheels whir in the Israeli's head. Ethiopia needs roads. Hippos block roads. Ethiopia doesn't need hippos.

Israel needs meat. Hippos are meat (and teeth). Israel needs Hippos!

A hurried cable is dispatched to the coalition government in Jerusalem. An emergency cabinet meeting is called. The Minister of Religion makes his report.

Yes, gentlemen, hippos have been certified to be kosher by the chief rabbinate. All bedlam breaks loose. The cries of joy are stifled only by the furious activity. The Foreign Ministry is cabling Washington for hippo canning experts. The Ministry of Commerce and Industry is drawing up bids on hippo-handling boats. The Defence Ministry is working on schedules of whole hippo convoys from Eilat to Beersheva. A cable goes out to the road expert in Addis Abba to return home for the awarding of a productivity prize.

Then the awful thing happens. A short, puffy, bearded man runs up to the Minister of Religion, whispers in his ear, writhes in anguish, and slinks away.

All eyes turn to the Minister of Religion. He rises slowly, supporting himself on his chair.

"Gentlemen, gentlemen," he says. "Word has just reached me that despite a thorough search of all the religious functionaries of the African and Asian immigrant communities, we have been unable to locate a single *shochet* (ritual slaughterer) who knows how to slaughter hippos."

Two days later the government falls. The public is informed that a disagreement on a vital security matter has made the present coalition untenable.

A day before the new elections are held, a small boy passing the government printing office picks up the charred remains of a can label on which "Hippos from the Holy Land" could clearly be made out. The Jewish Agency pays the fare for a one-way ticket for him and his family to America, build a special *shikun* in the Bronx to house them, and send the family to an Ulpan to learn English.

BANKS

Some months ago when I worked in a large office building in Tel Aviv, the office in the floor below us was let to a new firm. Painters, plasterers, carpenters, and miscellaneous laborers soon besieged the place. Under their onslaught it turned from a dingy, shabby hole into a modern office of, if not majestic, certainly not modest proportions.

Our curiosity as to the eventual occupants was whetted even further when we began to see the furniture being moved into it. There is some production-line office furniture made in Israel, and although it is functional, it certainly is primitive by American standards. This furniture, however, was gorgeous. It reeked wealth.

A few days later a gilded sign was inscribed on the door and the reason for the ostentation became obvious — a new bank was being opened in Israel.

Banks in Israel proliferate like fleas. Drive through the poorest, most squalid, new immigrant town and there, smack in the center, in all its modern architectural glory, will be the newest branch of Bank Leumi, the successor to the original Zionist Bank founded fifty-odd years ago. And chances are, if there are more than ten families in the town, this bank has one of its numerous competitors located across the street or down the block from it.

The smaller the bank, the more imposing its name. Chances are the "Israel International Trade and Commerce Bank" will be a hole in the wall in Jaffa run by two wealthy Iraqi brothers.

Banks in America lend money. If they do this in Israel, it is a very well guarded secret and occurs only under duress or lapse of sanity. Even when it does occur the interest rate charged is so astronomical that one is staggered by the figure.

If the banks in Israel don't lend money, they certainly make money. The papers are always full of explanations by economists as to why the country is in such a fix and why the banks are so well off.

I think it was George Bernard Shaw who said that if all economists were laid end to end, they still wouldn't reach any conclusion. Well, if the economists in Israel were laid end to end, they would certainly reach from the biblical Dan to Beersheva.

One thing anti-Semites in many lands always dote upon is how much of the country's banking is directed by Jews. At least in Israel, they would be almost right. With the exception of a lost Arab or two and that long arm of England, Barclay's, all the banking in Israel is in Jewish hands! Terrifying.

GEDULD ET. AL. VS. THE INTERIOR
MINISTRY OF ISRAEL

It took the children of Israel forty years of wandering and privation in the desert before the Lord found them fit to bring into the Holy Land. In keeping with this tradition and adapting it to our faster, modern age, the present government of Israel gives the newly arrived Western immigrant at least forty days of *tzorot* (like trouble but, more so) before he is allowed to remain here.

There is a widely publicized statement that the Israeli government's official policy is to encourage Western immigration. Yet underneath this facade lurks the terror in the average Israeli politician's heart that if this policy should succeed, where would they go to get money for their next election campaign? Consequently, there has arisen in this land of checks and balances a hidden but effective Committee for the Discouragement of Western Immigration. It works stealthily and underground, but its odious purpose soon becomes obvious.

It all became clear some hundred air miles before Israel when we were filling out our entrance forms. I am the possessor of a rare bundle — five genuine American passports. Even little David, aged one and one-half, had his. The reason for this is in case Papa has to come home on business and wants to leave the kids in Israel.

Anyway, on the entrance forms it says in three languages that one form should be filled out for each passport. I asked the stewardess, who I now know was the long arm of the committee, for additional forms.

"You don't need them," she said.

"Okay," said I, being a hater of paperwork.

Act I, Scene II
Passport Check at the Airport

Foreground: One irate father filling out four additional entrance forms.

Background and Chorus: Three howling children, one frantic wife.

The Committee has begun its work.

JACKALS

I've only seen them once. I was driving down a country road when my headlight beams caught two streaks of bushy-tailed, furry, dog-like beasts scampering across the road at fifty kilometers an hour.

I have heard them incessantly since I've been here.

Among the multitude of books I read about Israel before I came here was one about the flora and fauna of the country. Reading this book, I got the impression that the country was crawling with wild animals. The author, whose name I have forgotten, was not Jewish. I remember thinking at the time, What can he know about Israel? Quite a bit, quite a bit. Not only is the country crawling with wild animals but at night you would think they are all crawling next door.

I remember vividly the first night we spent in our new home. Our furniture hadn't arrived and we were sleeping on a few pieces of rented junk. Since Israeli homes have tile floors, the smallest sounds reverberate through an empty house like a properly designed hi-fi.

Night falls swiftly in Israel. In winter especially, it may be light at 4:30 and by 4:37 almost pitch black. Night fell quickly that first night in October. We finally got our three children tucked away in their makeshift beds and settled down into our straw-filled Israeli version of the sofa bed.

It is almost impossible to describe the nerve shattering impression one gets when he first hears the jackal's cry. We heard it that night and the hair on the nape of our necks bristled.

Perhaps Jeremiah composed the Book of Lamentation while sitting in the wilds of Judea listening to the jackals howl. No more appropriate background could be found. The oscillating wail sounds like a dying soul bemoaning its fate at the gate of hell.

It begins usually just after sundown. One lone voice breaks

the night's stillness with a wail of despair. It is quickly followed by an ever growing chorus of evil from all parts of the night. Suddenly, as if by some prearranged conductor's signal, there is complete silence. Even the crickets are still. Then slowly the insect sounds return and the night is at peace.

There is a formula by which you can tell the approximate temperature from the number of cricket chirps per second. Jackals are not so scientifically inclined. The rising and falling of their wails seems to follow no set pattern. They may howl once a night, almost continuously, or not at all.

As with everything else, they soon become such a normal part of everyday country living that we never even notice their presence unless we happen to have a tourist or Tel Avivian guest at our Jackal Acres.

SIGNED AND SEALED

Maybe it's just because I am writing this after Yom Kippur when many of the prayers are concerned with being "signed and sealed in the Book of Life," but somehow I have become quite seal conscious lately. Frankly in Israel its hard not to become seal conscious.

Last night I opened a bottle of orange juice concentrate. It involved not only unscrewing the cap, but also cutting a wire and lead seal on the neck of the bottle. I admit that Israeli orange juice is a kingly drink, but seals? The only places I can remember breaking seals on American products were on cigarettes and playing cards, for tax purposes.

The Hebrew preoccupation with seals goes way back. One of my neighbors is an amateur — no, rescind that — a semiprofessional (everyone in Israel is an amateur) archeologist. He has an exceedingly valuable collection of ancient coins and medallions from around 300 B.C.E. until the later Roman periods. Among his artifacts is a rather nondescript black coin. Ah, but hold it up to the light. Under transmitted light it glows a lovely purple and reveals the amber seal of one of the Maccabean kings.

Alas, if future archeologists ever dig up contemporary Israel, they will not find any lovely amber seals. Since Goodyear only got busy a century ago, I do not know for certain if they will find any seals at all; but if rubber lasts through the ages, the Israeli tells of the future will be strewn with hundreds of rubber seals, or *stempels*, the rubber stamps without which Israel would cease to exist.

It is absolutely impossible to conduct government business or any quasi-business function without being the proud possesser of a rubber seal. To illustrate:

Want to cash your paycheck? No good if just the boss signs it. He's got to seal it too with his faithful rubber stamp.

Customs official O.K.'s your declaration and initials it? Uh-uh, got to trudge back to the last warehouse in the port and get him to stamp his initials.

Buying a record book from the health ministry to record poisonous substances purchased? Be prepared to spend at least a half-hour stamping every cotton-picking page with the ministry's own stamp.

No one has estimated the millions of pounds spent annually for stamps, stamp holders, and stamp pads. In every new hamlet (oops, that's a bad word here) in Israel after the most necessary enterprise, the bank, sets up shop, the next most likely entrepreneur is the rubber stamp and seal dealer.

Rubber stamp republic? You bet!

DAVID'S DECIMAL SYSTEM

For the people of the book, Israel has pitifully few libraries. I have as yet been unable to determine the reason for this. Maybe the state was created too late for Andrew Carnegie or perhaps you cannot fight off Arabs with books. Anyway, this has led to a peculiarly Israeli phenomenon, the "involuntary lending library."

It begins when your new neighbors drop in to visit you. They gaze at the American furniture, ooh and ahh a little at the gadgets on the stove, and then, chances are, gravitate to your bookshelf.

Depending on their degree of biblio-addiction, they merely gaze at the titles or lovingly caress the covers. Then the questions begin. No one ever comes out and asks: "Can I borrow this book?"

First questions of policy must be determined. The opening of negotiations usually commences with: "How do you feel about lending out your books?"

What do they mean, How do I feel? I feel lousy! I'm one of those guys who treasure books above, beyond, or at least next to my wife. No one has asked me to lend her out — yet. Why ask me about my books?

Or: "What's your policy about people borrowing your books?"

Policy? Who has a policy. I don't even have a desire!

Do I answer with a flat refusal? Never. I usually stammer: "Well, sure if you take good care of them, I don't mind, heh heh. Anytime you want a book, just drop over, yes, drop over."

Is this passing invitation forgotten? Never. A few nights later, our neighbor rings our bell and enters with the announcement: "I've come to get something to read."

Unfortunately, my present neighbor's tastes run to Edgar Lee Masters, sex, detective stories, sex, and other profound reading matter of which I am fortunately woefully short. After two or three visits, he has exhausted my meager stock of semi-erotica and must search elsewhere down the road.

Speaking of searching, the other night I told my wife: "Say, I'm going down the road to get something to read."

My neighbors, it turns out, have lovely libraries, shelf after shelf of appealing books — in Hebrew. Ulpan anyone?

WHEN IT'S RAINING HAVE NO REGRETS

The most obvious thing about the rain in Israel is that most of the time there isn't any. From April until September nary a drop falls from Dan to Eilat. Once in a while you get some oppressively hot day and storm clouds gather on the horizon. You stand there expectantly, waiting for the first drops of cooling rain to fall and break the spell. It's a waste of time. It never does. It rains in the winter . . . period.

The first rain is usually greeted like a long delayed lover. People beam with joy and walk out hands outspread to greet the heavenly gift. After awhile, however, the gift wears out its welcome. It begins raining in earnest. Huge pounding drops bombard your clay tile roof with the sound of a boy dropping a pocketful of marbles on the floor. Lightning cascades across the Judean hills and bombards the countryside with a ferocity unknown to the Midwestern American.

Lawns wash away, roads are flooded, towns stranded, and dead, dormant river beds suddenly become twisting, terrifying torrents as waterfalls cascade along the wadis. And then — suddenly — it's dry. The sun bursts out like a giant flare. Its long rays, grasping fingers, seem to gather up the waters.

Rain in Israel is generally a local affair. If it's raining in Tel Aviv, it's probably not raining in Lydda eight miles away. From any high vantage point you can see the rain clouds skip and skirt over the land, sprinkling here, dousing there, like some giant celestial watering can.

There are a few really miserable rainy days when a constant cold drizzle engulfs the landscape. However, even on these days, I'm reminded of the aristocratic Italian-Jewish elevator operator in the building in Tel Aviv that housed our first office in Israel. Whenever one of his passengers had the audacity to complain of the wet weather he'd counter with the more prevalent Israeli attitude. "Rain — complain — rain *zot he brachah* — rain is a blessing."

ADVENTURE IN ABSTRACTION

For countless generations Jews had shunned the plastic and graphic arts because of the biblical injunction against producing graven images. This past lack of creativity is rapidly being made up for in the modern world, and especially in Israel. The Israeli landscape is littered with artists, mostly mediocre, a few good, and perhaps one or two great. There is much to paint in Israel and many willing hands to put it down on canvas.

Along with the profusion of painters, there are a plethora of art salons which dot Ditzengoff, Allenby, and Ben Yehuda streets in Tel Aviv and the main thoroughfares of Haifa and Jerusalem. Most of them are in surprisingly good taste, crowded but not overwhelmingly so, and a few are museums in miniature with superb displays. Usually they handle the work of a number of artists with a major exhibit devoted to one particular painter, but there are exceptions.

As an amateur assassin of the abstract whom the world as yet has not chosen to recognize (I was offered I£ 75, which sounds a lot more expensive than $25.00, for one of my famous paintings), I have always had the desire to rent a little store somewhere and display my own wares. This is precisely what certain Israeli artists have done and the results are catastrophic.

There is one such self-displaying art store, a 5-square-meter hole on Ben Yehuda, which particularly catches my attention. The pictures, all avant-rearguard abstract, are an abomination, but the frames, the frames are a joy to behold. Ten minutes in this store and I was a confirmed frame-gazer.

I would imagine it requires a considerable amount of *chutzpah*, to go into an art salon and ask for the frame instead of the picture and this is probably the reason why the store has no customers. The owner-artist couldn't care less about lack of customers. Every month her two meters of choice Tel Aviv frontage increases in value another 10 per cent. Here in the blessed Holy Land, she may someday soon retire, one of the world's wealthiest, lousiest artists.

BIBLICAL WATERMELON PATCHES

One of the three great agricultural festivals of the Jewish year, Succoth, is the time of ingathering of the fruits, when Jews are commanded to dwell in booths for eight days. Nowadays, even among orthodox Jews, the "dwelling" consists of simply eating meals in the booth, or *succah*.

Traditionally, the booths are a reminder of the temporary dwelling of our ancestors during the exodus from Egypt and until our arrival in Israel. We had no reason to question the source of this tradition. Now my wife has come up with her own interpretation. It all began with watermelons.

There is a large field at the foot of our street and soon after the spring planting immense creeping vines started to appear. Being dyed-in-the-wool city folk, we could only speculate on the nature of the finished product. We didn't have long to wait. In about four or five weeks, baby buds became baby *bulbes* (Yiddish-American for ball-like growths of diverse functions) and in a few more weeks nascent watermelons appeared on the vines.

In America, watermelons grow and grow and grow. In Israel they just kind of expand to the size of a kid's balloon and are ready for picking.

During the final few weeks of ripening, there appears on the edge of any substantial watermelon field a very peculiar structure. Four large poles about eight to ten feet long are driven into the ground to form a rectangle about four by nine feet. A platform is erected about halfway up the poles, and on this minature watchtower, a recumbent Arab spends his days and nights gazing at, and guarding the precious melon crop.

If he is an industrious or overly hot guard, generally the latter, he will soon erect for himself a top to his platform and cover it with leaves and straw. Then, to while away his time, he will construct canvas or straw walls and occasionally even a door.

By the time the melon crop is harvested, the countryside is dotted with some of the most genuine booths, or *succot*, any observant Jew would dream of erecting.

"Thou shalt dwell in Tabernacles for eight days."

Maybe you don't have to live in Israel to interpret the Bible, but it certainly helps.

CRICKET PICKERS

There are very few magazines in the world in which the advertisements are of more interest than the articles. *Scientific American* is one of these. In one of the fascinating ads I read many years ago, there was a formula for determining the temperature from the number of cricket chirps per minute. It seems the hotter a little ol' cricket gets, the faster it chirps. Crickets in Israel chirp like mad, and equipped with the formula for temperature cricket-chirp relationship, an amateur naturalist could find endless employment here.

About the only time I gave any thought to crickets in America was when the biannual revivals of *Pinocchio* came around and Jimminy got into the news. Here in the Israeli countryside, you don't need *Pinocchio*. Your ears tell you you're living in a veritable cricketeria. For a little country, the crickets in Israel are enormous. The average is about 48 millimeters in length, which is a good 2 inches of solid chirp.

Israeli homes, although generally hearthless, have ceramic tile floors and all-plaster walls and ceilings. When a 2-inch cricket crawls into this artificial echo chamber, the noise can be terrifying.

Maybe it is the *Pinocchio* syndrome, but for some reason I tend to be kind to crickets. I will, with no compulsion and usually with relish, squash any ant, centipede, fly, spider, and scorpion that invades our domicile, but the music lover in me somehow tempts me to spare that cricket.

Luckily I have a very fascinating wife. Among her many attributes that I was not aware of at the time of our marriage is her amazing adeptness at being an expert cricket picker. She'll reach under the furniture, grab the cold, slimy things with her bare hands, gently reprimand them for playing out of place, and then chuck them out-of-doors.

Before I came to Israel, I was offered all kinds of useless

advice on what to do, bring, etc. Let me state here a most useful fact for the prospective immigrant. If you're going to settle in the country, make sure someone in the family is an expert cricket picker.

THINK METERS

One of the finest legacies the American Industrial Revolution has left for mankind is the concept of indoor toilets and similar sanitary devices. As a result of this bequest, pipe sizes are measured in inches around the world. A piece of one-inch pipe drain is the same in Tennessee, Timbuctoo, or Tel Aviv, but there the similarity ends.

Everything else in Israel, as in most of the civilized world, is measured in meters. I've got to admit I fought learning the metric system, but to no avail. My collection of inch tapes is slowly ossifying in my toolbox and it has been replaced by a nice, cheap, effective combination inch-centimeter job and even on this I'm rapidly ignoring the inches.

Say you're building a closet with four doors and the space measures $74\frac{3}{16}$ inches. After a ten-minute session with second-grade fractions, which any normal American male forgets by the third grade, you come up with the dubious answer that each door should be 18 and 35/64 inches wide. This is all fine and good, but the average do-it-yourselfer has an unholy time trying to measure off anything finer than one-eighth of an inch.

Let's start over again. Measure the distance on the metric scale. One hundred and eighty-four centimeters. Fine. Divide by four. Each door is 46 centimeters wide. Simple? Yes! Fast? Yes! American? No!

After years of brainwashing, the average American gets some idea of how long a foot is. Six-foot-two, eyes of blue means something, but 188 centimeters, eyes of blue?

The only way to think meters is to repeat over and over in your dreams: thirty centimeters is a foot, thirty centimeters is a foot.

This works out just fine until you see an ad in the English language Jerusalem *Post*.

Wanted: Mannikin   87 cm.
                          54 cm.
                          89 cm.
                   168-172 cm. high

Conversion tables anyone?

WHOLY

I'm sitting here on my side terrace looking at one of the most remarkable sights on the local landscape. Towering in front of me like some modern day miniature tower of Babel is a steel pipe symbol of man's boredom, a TV antenna.

There are two supreme attractions in this community: one is a huge monster of a house built to resemble nothing so much as an airplane hanger, and the other is my neighbors' TV antenna.

On a Saturday afternoon, cars slow down and motor scooters come to screeching halts, people point, gaze, and garble in multilingual wonder at this phenomenon of the Western World. Israel today has no television, but it does have a bevy of unpleasant neighbors who provide some pleasant listening and looking.

TV set ownership is divided both ethnically and geographically. Ethnically, an Israeli Arab is more apt to have a TV set than an Israeli Jew and, geographically, most of the sets are in Haifa or the upper Galilee where reception from Beirut, Cyprus, and on freakish occasions, Italy, is extremely good. Here in the Sheplah, or lowland strip of Central Israel, reception is so-so and requires a huge, expensive antenna.

Israel is doing its best to discourage TV ownership by imposing fantastic customs duties, license requirements, and purchase taxes on sets brought into the country. Despite this, there are perhaps ten- to fifteen-thousand sets in the country and they continue to pour into Haifa port.

Let's say you've finally gotten your license, transferred your currency, paid your purchase tax, luxury tax, stamp duties, customs duties, port authority fees, and clearing agent costs, and are the proud owner of an Israeli idiot box. What can you see on it? Well for one thing, Gamal Abdul Nasser in all his sartorial glory. Most of Nasser's speeches, dedications, parade reviews, etc., are beamed to his adoring public throughout the Middle East.

Then there are Egyptian movies. A fact scarcely known in America is that Egypt outranks Hollywood as a producer of films. Not in quality, although Hollywood has been no great shakes on movies of quality lately, but in quantity. The biggest disadvantage of Egyptian movies is that they're in Egyptian. Granted its a melodious Arabic tongue, but without subtitles one is likely to get lost in the Middle East intrigues that light up the scintillating screen.

Of course, there is always Abbot and Costello with Arabic subtitles. If you ever miss your favorite program in America and are a traveling man, don't worry. Chances are you'll see it two years later as new nations emerge into the TV jungle.

Speaking of emerging, Israel will finally break down and put in TV one of these days. Oh, it'll begin with educational stations alright, but in a short time it's sure to boomerang into a full-fledged copy of its American progenitor. In a few years you'll probably be able to tell what political party an Israeli belongs to by the channel he watches, WHOLY Jerusalem or WRED Haifa.

There's one program, however, that practically everybody in Israel is praying to see someday: old David and Gamal sitting down together and signing a treaty for peace in the airwaves and earth in this area.

TEE OFF ON APHRODITE

Many nations busy themselves with building up new things. Israel is one of the few which busies itself at the same time, and perhaps even more enthusiastically, in building up old things.

Take Caesarea. Here was a magnificent heap of rubble that in the time of Herod was perhaps the largest, most prosperous city in Israel. Before 1948, Caesarea was the place from which the archeologically minded Palestinian stole a Roman column to grace his doorstep or front lawn. Well let's be fair, perhaps even more were stolen after 1948.

About the only people who cared about Caesarea were some Bohemian Moslem fishermen who lived there in ruined homes built upon ruined homes, built upon ruined homes. The catch was pretty good and the Roman pillars made fairly decent places to anchor a boat.

After the War of Independence, the fishermen left for Bohemia, and Israel, concerned with the doubling of its population in two years' time, let the rubble increase upon the ruins. As soon as the fundamental needs of housing and defense began to be stabilized in the late fifties, Caesarea began to be unstable. Teams of government and university archeologists descended on the place and a glorious, if infamous, past was slowly dug out of the sand.

If a tourist visits Israel at two- or three-year intervals, he is always impressed by the new buildings popping out of sand dunes, the new cities in the wilderness, but what I feel is even more impressive is to see old things rise again out of the crumbling dust of the ages.

When we first came to Israel in 1959 as tourists, Caesarea was a mess. The famous old red marble statue of a Roman god, beheaded millennia ago by a fastidious head collector or overzealous Moslem idol hater, was still reigning over the place along with miscellaneous columns and mosaics, but all was neglect and confusion.

Two years of loving toil have produced some fascinating changes. A crusader's castle has risen from the rubble complete with ramparts, moats, balustrades, and arches. Young Israeli feet can now tread on ancient Roman streets where Rabbi Akiva, the great sage of the first century, walked while awaiting his martyrdom.

Not only streets, but squares, homes, and whole city blocks are being unearthed. It is one thing to unearth; it is another to display. Perhaps the Jewish thirst for knowledge has given us a museum consciousness. Whatever the reason, these relics are superbly restored, identified, and displayed.

Thanks to the Rothschilds, Caesarea is also the home of the first, only, and, many people hope, last golf course in Israel. Thus the archeologists searching for a piece of the past are joined by the harried businessman searching for peace of mind in the present.

JUST PASSING THROUGH

I remember as a boy taking the New York Central train from Cleveland to New York. When the engines finally got up to top speed we'd zip through one small town after another with barely enough time to read the signpost. In today's jet age, Israel is just another small town. It's so small that a modern jet fighter can whisk across the country, along the narrow coastal strip, in about fifty seconds. Going the long way from north to south takes a little longer, about fifteen minutes.

Because of its minuteness, Israel's air space is constantly being violated. One day a couple of Indian navy jet fighters got fouled up on their way home to Bombay and tried a Yiddish shortcut. Maybe since it was Shabbat they figured nobody would mind a sixty-second violation and they could take the quick road to Bagdad. They reasoned wrong. No sooner did they enter our wild blue yonder when they were pounced upon by two Israeli jets.

It was quite a Shabbat afternoon's fun watching the four planes, two Israeli and two Indian, circling round and round, ever closer, ever lower. Finally the Indians got the message and landed safely at Lydda airport. They were entertained royally, put up at one of Israel's finest hotels, their planes checked and refueled, and wished bon voyage the next day.

Luckily amateur aviation has not developed to any extent in our neighboring Arab countries or we'd have to build a regular airport fly-in for Saturday navigators.

OLD FAITHFUL OF THE SHEPHLAH

Every other five square miles in Israel has some special biblical, historical, or even pictorial designation. The flat plain coast near Tel Aviv is known in the Bible and today as the Shephlah. Like most of the coastal plain, it is a fertile but dry area, which has been turned into the proverbial milk-and-honey land by the miracle of the pump and pipe.

As long as I can remember, Israel and dryness have been synonymous. If an American magazine runs an article about irrigation or land reclamation, it usually mentions Israel. If there is a TV show on the growing water shortage in America, Israel will get its share of the billing. With all this emphasis on the scarcity of water, what an astonishing sight it was to see one morning a huge geyser spouting in the fields about a mile off the Lydda airport road.

The water rose to a height of perhaps 30 feet and fell back into a perfect cascade of glistening diamond-like prisms as the hot morning sun pierced the column. Had a latter day Moses struck at a rock with his staff to create this deluge? Hardly. As I soon found out, a water pipe in the irrigation system had burst.

Old Faithful in Yellowstone erupts on schedule every thirty minutes. Old Faithful of the Shephlah isn't that punctual, but in the past month, I have seen it or its sister geysers erupt three or four times.

For a country where water is theoretically as precious as blood, Israel is one of the biggest water wasters around. I doubt if you could walk through more than three houses in any area of Tel Aviv without encountering a dripping pipe or water faucet. One governmental agency in a spirit of patriotism put out a "Save Water" poster some time ago that showed a large dripping faucet oozing away the country's watershed. I think this advertising scheme backfired because instead of heeding the written message on the poster, every public and private enterprise in Israel seems to be emulating the pictorial message and installing identical drippy faucets.

About the only remedy would seem to be one that would affect the pocketbook. When Israeli water prices go up to the Hong Kong level, perhaps there will be a local run on plumbers and washers.

SHIVERING AT THE SEASHORE

November is winter in Israel. By the manager's order, ties are worn in the offices of Bank Leumi and have been since October 15. Sweaters, blankets, and winter clothing are aired, kerosene vendors are hustling, and the beaches have been closed for six weeks. Is it cold? No. The temperature at noon in Tel Aviv is a lovely 93° and the sun streams down out of a cloud flecked sky.

The lovely beaches from Ashkelon to Nahariya are deserted, except for two specific groups of inhabitants. First, and in the minority, are the kooks and muscle boys, homebred and European imported. They are busy masochistically mauling themselves with their fists, touching their knees with their elbows, yogaing their way into all kinds of contortions and living the healthy life to the utmost.

The second group of denizens of the edge of the sea are the tourists; they abound in summer, proliferate in spring, and now are beginning to bloom in winter. The Scandanavians, the Germans, the English, the Americans, sit there on the sagging deck chairs near the Tel Aviv Hotel strip soaking in the lovely hot sun after invigorating dips in the cool, but not cold, water.

The Israeli man of the street, and there are many, will stop, stare, and if the view is right even ogle, but will he join them? Never! It's winter. Who goes swimming in winter? Maybe in Eilat, possibly in Tiberias, but in Tel Aviv . . . never.

The Jewish people have always been a calendar-conscious group. In biblical times, fires were lit on mountaintops and special messengers were employed to signal the appearance of the new moon and to regulate the months for religious reasons. Calendar mania seems to have rubbed off, and as soon as the Succoth holiday ends in September all public beaches are officially closed.

Ninety, schminety, it's winter, bring out the sweaters.

II

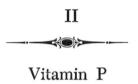

Vitamin P

MECHES ENGINEERING

Even the most illiterate Hebraist who comes to settle in Israel soon learns to know, pronounce, and hate, one word, *meches*. *Meches* means "customs," but it also means much more than that: it means arguments, endless forms, hot, sticky waiting rooms, overworked officials, and above all trivia, trivia, trivia, the most ridiculous outlandish bureaucratic trivia that Jewish genius can devise.

Customs duty is supposed to bring in revenue to the State. It may bring in money, but it drives away people. If the anti-Zionist American Council for Judaism wants to increase its membership, just let it get ardent American Zionists involved with Israeli customs.

Not even the high and mighty are exempt. I have seen top military brass stand by helplessly and sheepishly in the customs warehouses as the junior officials and their hatchet men hacked away at their belongings.

The Israeli customs officials are in the main decent God- and Government-fearing human beings with infinite patience and often the milk of human kindness. They are, however, bound by an ever changing collection of rules, regulations, and mores, which border on insanity.

Illustration: A returning member of the Israeli diplomatic corps is allowed to bring into Israel, duty-free, a washing machine he has used while abroad. A friend of mine made the mistake of keeping his washing machine in excellent condition despite four or five months use. The unit looked so good to the customs official that my friend was forced to bring down a panel of professors from the Mechanical Engineering faculty of the Haifa Technion to state that, in their opinion, the unit was not new.

The incidents involving personal goods pall to insignificance when one begins importing for manufacturing purposes. I am repelled from writing about them lest I blaspheme the State of Israel. Suffice is to say that in this new land a whole new field of engineering has been created, "Meches Engineering." All we need now is for some generous American donor to endow a new faculty at the Technion. Perhaps Lessing Rosenwald . . .

FLIES

One of the most remarkable entomological facts of our tourist stay in Israel four years ago was the absence of flies, fleas, and similar winged creatures. We stayed at hotels in Jerusalem, Herzliya, and Haifa, all with open, screenless windows and balconies, yet nowhere can we remember being pestered by flies.

When we remarked about this flyless Israeli life at a party in Detroit, where some Israelis were present, we were met with incredulous stares.

"No flies in Israel?"

"Where did you stay?"

"Never!"

We scoffed at their incredulity. We knew better. We had been there recently and there were no flies.

We are now, swat, in Israel, swat, as potential immigrants. Israel does not have flies. It has multitudes, swarms, and coveys of every conceivable winged creature known to the insect world, and although my neighbor may challenge this, swat, statement they are all in my house at the, swat, present time.

There is no way to live with flies in Israel. There are several ways to live without them. One, the flyswatter, develops tremendous biceps, but it has the disadvantage of being only limitedly effective on population reduction.

Two, *Time* magazine, folded to the movie or theater section and applied with a wrist-snapping action has a tremendous fly eradicating effect.

Third, the vacuum cleaner. This marvel of American productivity guzzles flies, fleas, dust, and spiders without discrimination.

Our own secret weapon against these beasts is a hungry cat. I have seen our Mitzi catch and gobble about eight flies in a minute as an appetizer before his morning meal.

The biggest unsolved mystery in our minds is what kind of agreement the Government Tourist Office has with the entomological distribution board.

KEEP THOSE BOTTLES QUIET

Israel has one great natural resource, sand. It covers two-thirds of the country in dunes, mountains, and sometimes just little piles. One of the basic constituents of glass is sand, so glass should be cheap and available in Israel. Available it is, but cheap . . .

Where else in the world does every housewife religiously collect every empty bottle she can lay her hands on? Mustard jars, jam jars, pickle jars, wine bottles, ketchup bottles, bleach bottles, all these wonderful items that form such a significant percentage of the rubbish heap in America are in Israel carefully washed and used again and again, until they are chipped so badly they will not close or stand.

Next to every home in our village is a small mound of empty bottles. One can tell the affluence or, in more cases, the indifference of the owners by how large a pile of bottles is allowed to accumulate before they are redeemed.

The small local supermarket contains an area equal to the size of the market that is a glassblower's dream. From floor to ceiling it is piled with short bottles, squat bottles, thin bottles, ugly bottles, and also, alas, broken bottles.

To make matters worse, not very much of any one thing comes in any one bottle. Pop, which is consumed in staggering quantities, is dispensed in peanut-sized bottles of 200 cc. each. Now 200 cc., as any good chemistry student knows, isn't much more than six shot glasses. On a real hot day I have counted twenty-three assorted empty bottles gathered in our bottle corner awaiting transfer outside.

To be fair one must admit that *mitz* (which is Israeli orange juice and very good) comes in quart bottles, but in this orange infested country the kids guzzle *mitz* like water and a quart goes fast.

What one could really use around here is a nice American-sized bottle of cola. But both Pepsi and Coke have long since succumbed to the Arab boycott, and Israel is one of the few free countries where a Coke sign is nonexistent. [Progress note: Among the spoils of the six-day war was a Coca-Cola bottling plant and trilingual coke signs now proliferate.]

Whereas we now go down to the beach to dig for old coins, future generations will unearth a legacy of bottle fragments.

WANTED: A GOOD JEWISH JUNKMAN

When we lived in a small town in southern Minnesota, there was only one Jew who had lived there before us, a junkman. This occupation, which for generations has been in Jewish hands in America, is, oddly, almost nonexistent in Israel. It's not that with the emergence of the "new Jew" in the redeemed land this Diaspora occupation has been looked down upon, but just plain ordinary old economics: in this Jewish land there just is no market for Jewish junk.

Of course, there is the famous "steel city" rising in Acco, but the basic raw material is — you should excuse the expression, pig iron. Floating junk to America or to America's old junk customer, Japan, has been thought of, but it is somewhat less profitable than shipping citrus.

So what happens here in this growing, rapidly industrializing country with the scrap steel, iron, sheets, angles, wire, boxes, bricks, boards, etc., that this type of economy produces? It just lays there.

Where?

Everywhere!

Anyplace there is industry in Israel there is a junkpile. On one of my first visits to Israeli industry I sat in the manager's office of a brand spanking-new tool-making concern in the Negev. The place was an architectural wonder with suspended ceiling, suspended concrete beams (and, unfortunately, as is the case so often, suspended production). Glancing through the window, we saw a door open and two supervision-type personnel walked out carrying a large box. Within full view of the manager's office, they unceremoniously kicked the box over and littered the landscape with assorted wood, paper, metal scraps, and general and miscellaneous *shmutz*. Today, that plant is probably buried in its own rubble.

Israel is dotted with large mounds, or tells, which are the

archeological remains of cities and civilizations whose rubble piled up upon themselves and in many cases were eventually abandoned. Perhaps this is what Khruschev meant when he said to America, "We will bury you." With the sons of America's Jewish junkmen rapidly becoming dentists, America may soon need to find new rubble rousers.

For most of Israel's myriad problems, there seems to be an American committee or organization that worries about them and pumps money into the country for a solution. Alas, no one seems to be worrying about Israel's junk and it is accumulating unchecked. But at least, thankfully, it is hidden from the average tourist's view.

Who knows, perhaps someday a Zionist junkman will set up a nonprofit smelting operation and incinerate the mess.

OH BEAUTIFUL FOR CLEAN-CUT LOOKS

One of the things that an American living in a foreign land begins to notice very acutely is his fellow Americans. The literary-movie-press concept of the contemporary American as a tall, healthy, well-dressed, clean-cut, slightly extrovert, friendly personality is something no one feels, thinks about, or even, frankly, often sees in the States. In Israel, those qualities stand out like sore Yankee thumbs.

I was in the luxurious lobby of the Dan Hotel in Tel Aviv one delightful November day during a convention of the International Junior Chamber of Commerce. Standing near the post-office window I heard the deliciously rich, cornpone-dripping overtones of a pure Georgia accent saying: "You'all don' really mean its goin' to cost eight powands to ship that to the States?"

What a lovely sound after months and months of perfect British English or pluperfect South African English.

As I gazed upon the lobbyful of successful American J.C.'s, it struck me how much like his caricature the typical American really is. Tall, they stood out like corn stalks among the clover. Healthy, they had a glow of good health about them that even seemed to overshadow any residual alcoholic coloring. Well-dressed, like pages out of the *New York Times Sunday Supplement,* the well-dressed look that goes with mass-produced clothes. Israeli businessmen are rapidly becoming clothes-conscious, and the "Impeccable Israeli" is rapidly overtaking the "Kibbutz Cut." Yet Israeli tailoring is still mostly custom-made and lacks the look of democratic affluence that American clothes possess.

There are loud Americans, slovenly Americans, obnoxious Americans, and once in a while a few disgusting Americans who make their way over here; but fortunately, Hollywood's perfect image seems to have rubbed off on many of our present generation and America is putting her best foot forward in the Middle East.

BRIEFCASES

Years ago every orthodox Jew carried his *talis zekle,* in which his prayer shawl and phylacteries were kept. This custom has been transformed into the modern Israeli practice of carrying a briefcase.

Stand on any corner in any town, and if you have a statistical mind, you'll soon discover that a minimum of 73.2 per cent of all Israelis over fifteen months are carrying some form of briefcase.

Since conformity in Israel is nonconformity, you may never encounter two similar briefcases. They have clasps and buckles, and pockets in pockets and on pockets, and zippers to zip zippers; they're rhomboid and trapezoidal, baggy and straight, cloth and, heaven forbid, pigskin, and the diversity knows no bounds.

And you can never win trying to correlate briefcase to owner. The bearded, earlocked Yemenite road laborer will carry an impressive semi-leather case chock-full of felafel, humus, and assorted oriental delicacies suitable for a Middle Eastern snack, whereas the president of a prospering new bank may be carrying a shredded worm-eaten relic of his long forgotten youth in Berlin.

The common building laborer is perhaps the most stalwart son of the briefcase brigade. The steel lunch pail, that social equalizer of the American labor scene is practically unknown in Israel. Instead, the Israeli partisans of socialist labor trudge to work with capitalistic briefcases bulging with bread, bottles, and bagels. Even the Arab workers have begun adhering to this status symbol and it is losing its essentially Jewish flavor.

For several days a most impressive monogrammed tan briefcase reposed in the corner of my office at work. Thinking that one of the building engineers who were working on the plant at the time or one of the myriad government officials who constantly descend upon us had left it there, I let it repose undisturbed, awaiting its owner. Finally after five days, my curiosity got the better of me. Tenderly I lifted the case to the table. It sagged slightly under an impressive burden. What sheaf of documents lay inside? What engineering or government secrets would pour from its hold? I snapped the lock open and gazed into the bowels of the briefcase. There inside, in all their primitive glory, were five full and half-filled paint cans, one stiff paint brush, and one semi-used wiping rag.

The first time I saw it was on the coastal road between Herzliya and Tel Aviv — a large sign with 30,000 on it and some, at that time, unintelligible words. I remembered similar signs back in Michigan that totalled the auto accidents in a particular county. Thirty-thousand auto accidents so far this year in Tel Aviv? Could be, could be.

Two days later we were sitting in a sidewalk café in Haifa when a man stepped over to offer us what looked like monopoly money. Not being in the market for play dough, we politely refused.

Later one of our multilingual companions explained: Israel has a national lottery. Tickets cost I£ 2.00 apiece. The grand prize is I£ 45,000 tax-free, with a host of smaller prizes ranging down to I£ 3.00, which pays for next week's ticket.

Mifal Hapayis, the name of this legal numbers racket, is a big, big business in the country. Ticket sellers are available and unavoidable everywhere. Whole store fronts in main business sections are filled with displays of last week's, last month's, or last year's coupons. They sell nothing else but chance and luck. There are permanent outdoor stands, temporary outdoor stands, stands with flashing lights, ticket sellers who operate from folding chairs and tables, and ticket sellers who operate from their back pocket.

Profits go into a hospital fund. No one I've asked seems to know the take, but it's estimated to be astronomical.

The drawings, which have managed to stay pretty much corruption free, are held every Thursday so the winners can have a nice weekend. Results are in all the papers and winning numbers are plastered all over town.

I've never met anyone yet who has ever seen a big weekly winner. They probably emigrate immediately upon payoff to avoid the hordes of *schnorrers* who must obviously descend upon them. To a Westerner the whole thing seems a little degrading and repugnant. I've only I£ 3.00 so far. Oh well, there's always next week.

EXPERT PASSION

If you're attracted to this because you think it might have something to do with sex, forget it. Perhaps this would be better entitled "Passion for Experts." Call it what you will, the Israeli government and the Israeli public have an awe for the expert that borders on the fantastic.

Per capita, there are probably more engineers, doctors, economists, scientists, etc., in Israel than any country in the Middle, Near, and Far East. Yet, if the Israeli government plans a new plant, plants a new crop, raises a new breed of chicken, or considers a scheme to bottle *gefilte fish*, they search the Western world for a foreign expert.

The farther or more foreign, the better. A Dutch expert is respected, an English expert honored, but an American expert is revered — at least for a while.

The first decline in veneration of the American expert takes place about a week or two after he arrives in the country. He's registered at the best hotel, has met some government big or semi-big wigs, has been whisked around the country, and has made the necessary courteous laudatory remarks on Zionist achievements. Then the fun begins. He starts to work on the job he was brought over to do.

"Based on the way we achieved the maximum productivity on this in the States, I'd say it would be better if you integrated your conveyors and operated the assembly line from a — .

"What! How can we do that in Israel?"

"The Histadrut wouldn't stand for that kind of a setup."

"We did it that way in Germany in 1933."

"It doesn't sound the least bit plausible to me. Now if you look at it from my point of view."

No government office admits to keeping statistics on how many experts leave during the first week, but the number who take solace in booze at the bar of the local hotel is legion. If he can survive the first few weeks, however, the battle is won.

Retribution is at hand however. Israel is now an overdeveloped nation and is sending her own experts to the burgeoning African, Asian, and Latin American nations.

The day will come when the Israeli expert arriving at work in Bulwayo will say: "Based on the way we achieved the maximum productivity on this in Tel Aviv . . .

VITAMIN P

Many years ago my mother gave me a little prayer book that contained the grace said after meals. It was issued by a now forgotten food company, and as part of the pitch to promote their products, they had in the front of the book a little history on the discovery and naming of vitamins. I remember practically nothing about it except that the discoverer and coiner of the word vitamin was a man with the unforgettable name of Casmir Funk.

This really has little to do with a discussion of Vitamin P, which is a strictly Israeli phenomenon, but at times the pedagogic urge in me is too strong to overcome. Vitamin P is an Israeli synonym for the Hebrew-Yiddish word *protectzia* — English translation, "protection, without it you are lost."

Let me illustrate the workings of Vitamin P. A good friend of mine, who has been courageously fighting the battle of integrating himself into Israeli society, became a new settler here for the third time. (Like many Americans, he found it easier to fight for Israel than to live in it.) On his last entry he was entitled to bring into the country, duty-free, one used television set. This invaluable item was purchased new in Germany and instructions were given for repacking in different boxes, removing labels, and generally aging the item. When the set was unloaded in the Haifa port and the moment of unveiling before customs arrived, lo and behold, the set emerged like a brand-new butterfly with all its labels and packing in its new cardboard cocoon.

Anyone who has not gone through Israeli customs cannot begin to invision the joy that radiates from a harassed customs official's overworked body when he catches a customs evader red-handed. My friend, who is quite small, was slowly trying to slink into the TV tube when the door opened and in walked a senior customs officer.

Now one of the best ways of acquiring Vitamin P is through marriage and it so happens that this customs official was a cousin-in-law to my friend. He sized up the situation in a microsecond and ceremoniously declared: "That's not a new TV set, any fool can see it's been used." With a choke of agony, the original customs inspector confirmed his "obvious" decision. Vitamin P had done its work well.

There is the apocryphal story about the thirty-year settler whose home had burned down. He had run almost two miles to a fire station. When the fire chief surveyed the ruins of his home with him, he asked why he hadn't reported the fire to the station only a block or so away.

"How could I," replied the old settler, "I didn't have any *protectzia* at that station."

HISTORICAL SITES

On the road to the Lydda airport are five huge hewn rock boulders. Nobody knows how they got there, who erected them, what part they played in the War of Independence, or what historical connection they have with early Judaism. *Thank God!*

ALL THAT IS ORANGE IS NOT EDIBLE

Not too far from our home on the crest of a gently slop-
ing little hill, there rises the magnificent home of one of the
wealthiest printers in Israel. Aside from the more prosaic
everyday items his company prints, such as radio tax forms and
compulsory loan tax forms, it is also the principal printer of a
hideous little item known as the purchase tax stamp.

To call it a stamp is to make a mockery of philately. It
is a nondescript blob of bright orange cellophane-like paper
with a black number on it. It is affixed on anything and everything, except food, in Israel by some transfer-like mechanism
similar to the bubble gum transfers we used to put on our arms
when we were kids.

The versatility, flexibility, and universality of these little devils
is overwhelming. We have been living in our new home for five
months and are still battling the stamps. They are on the
faucets, the toilet seats, the door knobs, the drawer pulls, the
light fixtures, everywhere. When we just moved in, the place
looked like a Halloween harlequin nightmare.

Practically everything made in Israel crumbles at the touch:
plastic dishes shatter on the tile floors, children's furniture cor-
rodes before your eyes; but purchase tax stamps — they, like the
Jewish people, are indestructible. You can wash them, scrub
them, rip them, tear them, scrape them, peel them, and they
won't budge. It's better to just ignore them.

There are two stamps on a ceramic towel hanger in our
bathroom. I have spent considerable time scratching, scraping,
and clawing at the stamps. My only symbol of success has been
a slight amount of orange residue cached under a sore finger-
nail.

Some months ago we bought a five-hundred-kilogram scale for
our plant. Just before we received it and loaded it onto our truck,
a functionary of the company bounded out of the shipping room

door with a huge sponge and reels of orange paper. He proceeded to envelop our scale with tax stamps which to this day remain a mute monument to bureaucracy and probably, incidentally, unbalance our scale.

KOIF EPP ESS

Frankly, I can't remember any peddlers in America. Oh, I know there were probably many, but I just can't remember. In Israel you can't forget.

Sit down in a nice restaurant in Tel Aviv. Not an expensive restaurant, a nice restaurant, *kosher, traif,* it makes no difference. Order your soup, your *kishke,* or your *gehachte lebber,* dip your fork in, and the next thing you'll hear is "*Koif eppess*" ("Buy something").

There are at least four regulars that frequent the stretch of Allenby Road where I usually eat: the pen-and-pencil man, the Mogen David woman, the Mifal Hapayis man, the Mr. Koif Eppess.

The pen-and-pencil man — he also does a thriving business in razor blades — is the most dignified. In a land of briefcases, his is semi-impressive. From every pocket and from his briefcase, he exudes pencils, leads, fillers, replacements, ink, and heaven only knows. He does a successful amount of business. Probably from inveterate napkin scribblers.

The Mogen David woman is the epitome of *hamishkeit* ("motherliness"). She is selling chances on eight cars to be auctioned off in the next millennium. Proceeds go to the Israeli Red Cross — oops, Red Star of David. Even if you have a wallet stuffed full of these chances, refusal to purchase an additional one results in a stare that chills the hottest goulash soup.

Mifal Hapayis, the National Lottery man, is just incredulous if you don't buy a two-pound chance. He just cannot see how a person who gambles with his health eating in the place is not willing to gamble with his pocketbook.

Mr. Koif Eppess is dear to my heart, and to my fender. (He ran directly in front of my car last week and I nearly enjoyed some peaceful meals.) In certain pygmy tribes in the Belgian Congo he would be considered a giant; in America he's about the size of a ten-year-old. But size be damned. He has the biggest pack of all: three or four ex-boyscout knapsacks bulging with some of the most useless junk I have ever seen assembled in one place, outside of the "fun" houses in the seedy downtown sections of U.S. cities. You can get whistles, dolls, toothpicks, bracelets, charms; in short, anything that Jewish and Japanese ingenuity can manufacture. Frankly, I have never seen him make a sale. Maybe his approach is wrong. His *"koif eppess"* is just too nasal.

I've just been approached by a new wonder in Israeli industry. The public relations man. Maybe I'll send him to see Mr. Koif Eppess; but then how could I ever eat in peace?

POLISHING UP THE TARNISH

After the Zionism has worn off slightly and you begin to realize that living in Israel is not vacationing in Israel and that making ends meet is a long arduous grind, there are some small things that come your way that make you realize it is still worthwhile.

There is an abandoned olive grove in back of our factory in Lydda — central Israel is full of abandoned olive groves — and in the middle of it is a dirt track leading, it seems, to nowhere. One morning as the sun was busy baking the landscape, an old, battered, time-worn wagon creaked and crept along the path. The wagon wasn't much nor was the horse, you see their likes every day in front of your bumper, but the driver was something special.

Most wagon drivers in Israel curse at their horses or mules in a multitude of picturesque languages, but this driver was singing the morning prayers in a beautiful tone, much more fit for the synagogue than the shay. I don't know if Jewish carriage drivers sang to their horses in Europe; I know I never heard a Jewish junkman singing in America. Even if they did, their song would appear hollow in comparison with the utter joy and complete faith which seemed to radiate from this thoroughbred troubadour.

Frankly, Lydda is a god-forsaken city that time, progress, and the United Jewish Appeal seem to have passed by. Of course there is a big new development area with whole new streets, apartments, and office buildings, but the overall impression is still one of poverty, filth, and neglect.

In the middle of one of the poorest sections, bounded by broken-down streets and even worse houses, there is a lovely little oasis of grass and green, the city park. We were sitting on our favorite park bench eating lunch the other day, when two little ragamuffins strolled by.

Lydda kids have a reputation for being, to say the least, wild. A cat, a bird, or even a stray dog doesn't stand much of a chance when set upon by these products of the Moroccan and Tunisian mellahs. Fact is, Israel kids in general don't have too high a rating when it comes to courtesy or respect of elders and animals.

As we watched the two lads approach, we thought what smart alec thing are they going to say or do now. Instead their faces brightened and with feeling and sincerity said, *"B'tay avone"* (*"hearty appetite"*).

Even my cynical three-times-back-and-forth-America-to-Israel companion was touched. A good appetite here, a little song there, these are the things that polish up the tarnish on one's Zionism.

ISRAEL'S NATIONAL BIRD

If the Israeli parliament sees fit to choose a national bird, it will agree in rare unanimity on the fowl that has played such a fundamental role here since the founding of the State, the chicken. If by some biochemical quirk, the body cells of a person could be traced back to their original food source, we could quickly determine that the Israeli population averages 82.3 per cent chicken. Probably no other people produces, prepares, and consumes chicken on the scale of the Israelis.

There are many reasons for this, historical, climatic, religious, but mostly economic. The price of the cheapest ground meat in Israel may be five times that of the cheapest chicken; so if a family is going to eat meat, it's the bird.

The chicken already enjoys quite a few honors and privileges in Israel. Although it is not a paid up member of any of the bus cooperatives, it enjoys the right to journey on these vehicles without cost and does so regularly in many communities. On a crowded bus the provocative peck a pretty girl may get on her posterior will most likely be avian and not humanoid.

Most chickens, however, are quite dignified on buses, usually more so than the biped passengers: they never smoke or spit and seldom crack sunflower seeds on the floor. If one lays an occasional egg while enroute, it is shrugged off as a misguided mission in maternity and quietly cleaned up by the flies or, on rare occasions, the bus company.

Some of the most fantastic factories in the country are devoted to the handling, picking, flicking, and packing of chickens. I visited an automated enterprise in Hadera where generations of feathered fowl make a cool exit from life as frozen chicken for export. From feathers to fleas, every part of the bird was utilized in one stage or another of the operation.

Contrasted to this multimillion dollar operation are the thousands of ritual slaughterers who practice in all the back alley nooks and crannies of Tel Aviv and the smaller towns. The old Thanksgiving cartoon of Daddy chasing the turkey with an ax is seldom emulated even in rural Israel, since most slaughtering is done by religious authorities.

Whether she brings it home cut, quartered, koshered, and frozen in her patent leather shopping bag or carries it live and squawking on her back, the Israeli housewife has truly made the chicken Israel's national bird.

VESPA VIRGINS

The vast difference between American and Israeli mores may be easily summarized by the reaction of the American woman and the Israeli woman to a common word used to describe their physical charms. Call an American girl "a piece" and you'll get slapped for it; call an Israeli girl a *chaticha* (translation: "a piece") and you'll get thanked for the compliment.

The Israeli girl has it, throws it, and shows it. The American has it, hides it, or bides it. The average male growing up in bosom-oriented pre- and post-war America is left a drooling, helpless, finger-biting wreck when exposed to Israel's womanhood. I have not seen any statistics correlating a country's area to its average bra size, but I'm sure if such a survey were made, Israel would win hands down.

The female form has become such a fruitful financial field that many foreign investors have been drawn to its support. The Israeli female can now have her choice of bras produced under American, French, or Italian license.

For one segment of Israel's population however, this investment has fallen flat. The overwhelming majority of Israel's Arab village women are content to keep things as they have been for generations and have not been enlightened by modern civilization.

Another intriguing phenomenon for the socially-conscious is what I call the Vespa Virgin Syndrome. In this country of limited means but large assets, a great deal of running about is done on Vespa scooters. If a female rides on this vehicle, she is forced to hoist her already abbreviated skirt to a high-watermark position, mount the sturdy steed, and hang on to her escort for dear life. My choice of the appellation Vespa Virgin is derived from the fact that the serious observer doubts that one can retain this condition when so overly exposed.

MEOWS

Along with the miracle of the ingathering of exiles here in Israel, another miraculous ingathering has occurred on a lower biological level — the ingathering of the cats. Feline historians vaguely locate the natal place of the domestic cat in Egypt. I think they were about two or three hundred miles off base.

A walk through Tel Aviv, or especially Jerusalem, will convince even the most skeptical that cats have returned to Israel en masse. I remember a particular evening a few years ago in Jerusalem when I strolled with a statistically minded friend. He kept his mathematical mind working by counting all the good-looking girls encountered in a half-hour's journey and I, not wanting to be so mundanely preoccupied, counted cats.

Cats far outnumbered girls. I recall noting 72 genuine species.

In a land of milk and honey, most cats in Israel are getting a raw — unfortunately not meat — deal. Maybe I lived in the wrong neighborhood, but I never saw a really hungry cat in the States. There always seemed to be enough garbage to go around.

In Israel it is different. The holy cats here are lean, mean, and hungry. Their gaunt bodies and bulging eyes make them look like Charles Adams' models.

I don't remember seeing American cats eat bread; in Israel they devour it. There's one restaurant in Tel Aviv near Rothschild and Allenby that is a cat's haven. Like many Israeli restaurants it has an outdoor garden. It's crawling with cats. Unless you are inured to it, you feel guilty about taking a bite with these beasts around.

Once I ordered some quasi-Arabic meat dish at this place. Completely inedible. Although I went hungry, my old cat lover's soul was refreshed as I watched the snarling felines devour my dinner.

Going home from the office one afternoon, my secretary, Pinina, and I encountered one of the most pathetic-looking cats

I have ever seen. Her neck (and my secretary is prepared to testify to this) was no bigger than my finger. The poor creature was the epitome of an old Yiddish expression my father liked to use, "*oisgedarte katz.*" Perhaps the closest English equivalent is "squeezed out cat."

Pinina took this miserable animal home and raised it for three weeks. She then turned it over to my five-year-old daughter Lisa, who still had fond memories of Snipsy, her St. James cat. Let's face it, Israeli cats are not American cats. In two days Lisa, Lonnie (three years old), and Toby (my wife, ageless) were covered with scratches and Merthiolate. The cat was covered with lice.

Well, Toby gave the cat two delousing baths, which silkened her fur but not her temperament. A couple of nights ago I was sleeping soundly when I felt sharp fangs gnawing on my finger. Crocodiles in Israel? Impossible. I snapped out of my dream in time to throw Snipsy II out of bed. David (one-and-a-half) has lately begun eating the cat's food. She's got to go!

DO LITTER

Buried in a review of a Japanese roadshow touring Tel Aviv was a comparison between Japan, the neatest country in the world, and Israel, the most untidy. Although this may mean my banishment from the Zionist Organization of America (I haven't paid my dues since I've settled here anyway; I mean, how Zionist can you get?), I must admit that this statement is 100 per cent correct.

Outside of upper Haifa, the wide open spaces, and, of course, where we live, the country is a mess. At one time paper was scarce in Israel; now you can pick up all you want at any street corner.

Kids in Tel Aviv play a game based on how many scraps of different foreign language papers you can find in a given time.

Everybody reads in Israel and a good part of the deluge of the daily papers drifts down to the streets, adding local color to the landscape. Along with twigs, string, bottles, candy wrappers, ice cream sticks, etc., any Israeli city can be outstanding in its population class for one of the world's messiest.

Things are being done about this. Things are always being done about things in Israel. But the untidiness does not only stem from litter. Buildings built just four or five years ago are going to ruin from lack of paint and maintenance. In fact, with the possible exception of good-looking women, camels, and cars which have certain above average values, everything else tends to look more or less disheveled.

There are many good reasons for this: the vast immigration of the past decade, the low wage scales, the preoccupation with building rather than rebuilding.

Perhaps a Hebraist will someday find a tongue-catching equivalent for litterbug and an effective cleanup campaign can be launched. Meanwhile, I'll continue to throw my unburnable trash on the lot across the street. Gosh, I hope someone doesn't start building there.

Some years ago I read a book on the history of beards. All I remember about it is the one passage that said if any people know how to wear beards with dignity, it is the Jews. That this book is right can readily be seen on any street in Tel Aviv, or perferably B'nai Brak or Jerusalem.

My discourse, however, concerns one of the poorest examples of dignified beards I have ever seen. It belongs to one of those enterprising gentlemen of upper Allenby Avenue who have passed through the twilight zone separating begging from free enterprise.

The word "character" has many connotations in the everyday world and all of them apply to this rugged individualist. His strong but worn and weary face peers out from a forest of hair. Hair on his head, hair on his cheeks, hair on his chin, hair engulfing his ears, all of it in a turmoil of confusion. He reminds me of one of those horror movie werewolves gone wild.

Now, hair on a human being is not necessarily a disfiguring or disgusting thing. In fact, millions are spent annually on panaceas to restore this commodity to the males who have lost it. But in our millennia of civilizations, we have developed the concept that hair must be oriented in some pleasing fashion to be acceptable. About the only things that have passed through this latter day Samson's hair have been dust and wind.

What prophetic message does this apocryphal figure cry out to the passing public as he stands there in all his shaggy glory? Some forecast of doom? Some damnation of sin? No, nothing as demanding as that. This Rasputin-like member of the Hebrew race is merely trying to peddle combs on the streets of Tel Aviv!

SQUEEZE

One of the grave dangers any prospective American emigrant to Israel must face is the chance that some morning he may wake up, grope his way into the bathroom, groggily wash his face, squeeze out his toothpaste on his toothbrush, and brush his teeth with hair cream or shampoo. These items, like dozens of others which are generally packed in plastic or glass bottles in the States, are packed in Israel, in soft toothpaste-like tubes.

Somehow I find it rather terrifying when I ask for the mayonnaise and I receive a huge toothpaste tube to squeeze out on my salad. Other household items, like mustard and the old Israeli oriental standby of humus (sesame-seed mishmash), also come in tubes.

You would think that with this tube-orientated industry you would have no trouble buying the equivalent of an American "giant-size" or "family-size" tube of toothpaste. No such luck. Mayonnaise yes, but toothpaste never. I guess people don't brush their teeth conscientiously or maybe they roll their own, because the average commercial Israeli toothpaste tube is good for only forty squirts.

After scraping the hair cream off my teeth one morning, I was comforted by the thought that it could have been worse: there in the medicine cabinet was another Israeli innovation — shoe polish, black, in tubes.

RIP VAN YANKEL

Any neighborhood in Israel provides a condensed geography lesson. Within home-run distance of my house live people from Argentina, Poland, Germany, Hungary, Belgium, Iraq, England, Czechoslovakia, Italy, Belgian Congo, but most of all South Africa.

The Jews of South Africa came there en masse about the turn of the century when most of their brothers and sisters emigrated to America. The majority of the South African Jews came from Lithuania and three generations of interplay between Lithuanian-Jewish scholarship, piety, and industriousness, and British finesse and gentility have produced a unique people.

Here is the antithesis of the impolite, impatient Israeli. The patience, the charm, the manners of the average South African immigrant are a joy to behold in a country where these attributes are just beginning to be redeveloped.

The contribution of South Africans to Israel has been outstanding. They have built cities, industrial companies, banks, and commercial enterprises of all kinds and have run them from here, not by proxy as so many American enterprises are.

One of their unique contributions to Israel however is bowling-on-the-green. In Savyon and Ramat Gan are two lovely bowling greens that would do credit to any English countryside. There on the verdant, immaculately clipped lawns, in equally immaculate white uniforms, can be found Jews from all the six continents and a few native Israelis quietly emulating Sir Francis Drake.

When the American Jews establish a few good baseball diamonds, then maybe we can feel we've arrived.

PHILATELICALLY SPEAKING

When President Shazar was inaugurated last year, nobody made much fuss. The kids in Jerusalem got out of school to wave at him and the overzealous artillery broke a few windows in the Knesset with their booming salutes.

But when a new Israeli stamp is issued — that is a different matter. Months before, feelers are sent out from the post office cautiously announcing the blessed event, artists are selected, competitions held, and finally, the design in all its glory is revealed to the public. Black-and-white prints appear in the papers and the stamp stores, and the date is announced officially in the philatelic birth section of all the major periodicals. Crowds jam the post office. At last the day is here.

The Israeli government is quite cautious about issuing a commemorative set of over three issues. A momentous occurrence of this type is enough to cause the fall of the cabinet if it does not come off smoothly.

I assume stamp collecting is universal, but in Israel it is ingrained. It is no exaggeration to say that there are as many stamp stores in a two-block area of Tel Aviv as there are in the entire city of Detroit. They occupy some of the choicest locations, and in a country where power is at a premium, many of them are air conditioned. Not only are they many but they are prosperous. I have actually seen a waiting line for a stool in one of the stamp stores on Allenby Road. Is this a kid's hobby? Far from it. The average age of the avid collector appears to be about forty-five. Many of the establishments are manned by gentlemen who look more like bank presidents. There are even exclusive stores that operate on the wholesale and/or auction market and won't talk to the ordinary collector.

Stamps used to be dingy depictions of obscure generals and statues, but since World War II many aspiring nations, Israel among them, have printed some beautiful, asthetically perfect issues. Every Israeli issue contains some stamps in the printed sheet that have a little descriptive tab attached with a meaningful, usually multilingual, statement about the stamp. Thus every Israeli stamp is collected double by the serious collector, the tabbed and untabbed variety.

This, however, still does not adequately explain the vast number of stamp stores in the country. It is probably a shrewd device thought up by the Treasury Department as an anti-inflationary measure. Regardless, a two-minute stroll in Tel Aviv will soon convince you that Israel is a postage-stamp republic in more than just size.

JUNIOR DAVIDS

One of the less constructive biblical legacies has been the preoccupation of a portion of the younger male generation with a modern version of King David's famous weapon, the sling. The giant killer has been altered with thick modern rubber bands and a Y-shaped olive branch. It closely resembles the good old American slingshot.

I first became aware of the predominance of this formidable weapon when a beautiful, large snow-white owl flew into the eaves of our factory. In hot pursuit, there emerged out of the olive orchard in back of the plant, a scraggle of urchins. In each of their tiny filthy hands they held one and sometimes two slingshots. Their zeal was better than their ballistics, however. The owl disdainfully rose and sauntered out of slingshot range.

Weeks later I finally traced down the anthropological reason for the predominance of slingshots in the Lydda-Ramle region. I was engaged in the popular Israeli road sport of dodging sheep and goats when a little Arab urchin stepped out near the car. Slipping a stone into his slingshot, he took careful aim and blop, a wayward goat was gently urged to rejoin the flock.

PLANES

I first saw an Israeli Air Force plane four years ago in Haifa when I was visiting Israel as a tourist. Strangely enough, I was standing on the balcony of the aeronautical engineering building of the Technion.

The view, for an old flatlands boy from the Midwest like myself, is staggering. The magnificent sweep of the Haifa bay area, its panoramic green, and its industrial heart is an unforgettable sight.

Suddenly, into the middle of this peaceful landscape, burst two tiny dots of motion, Israeli Air Force jets with Stars of David on their wings. I cried. Why? Maybe you can start with the now classical explanation for the success of the United Jewish Appeal. Start with two thousand years of persecution.

Yesterday was the fifteenth Independence Day of Israel and twenty-eight French (God bless them) Mirage Jet Fighters streaked across the country on the way to the parade in Haifa.

Later, our next door neighbor, a woman of the world in her fifties, came over to me and said, "You know, Chaim, when I saw those planes, I went into the bedroom and cried."

Why?

Try starting with two thousand years of persecution.

III

A Good Geves Man

Wanted:
A Good Geves Man

III

Wanted:
A Good Geves Man

How many times have you gone into a hardware store and had the proprietress remove a suckling child from her breast and wait on you? With all their gimmicks, I don't think any American stores have tried this one yet. In fact, there are probably not too many mothers in America who could breast feed their child at one instant and do a good job of cutting pipe the next.

The little store where this incident occurred is just ten short minutes away from our home. It might as well be ten worlds away. I remember how surprised I was when, moving from a rather homogenous home district in Cleveland, we settled in an area of Detroit where homes valued from $12,000 to $100,000 could be found within a block of each other. It was good conditioning for Israel. Not only are the homes twenty price ranges apart but the people are twenty millennia apart.

In the same evening I can walk to an oriental wedding feast, where toothless hags crumbled by decades of childbearing and labor are trilling out an ear piercing shriek (lu, lu, lu, lu), to a recital of a violin string quartet held in a baronial mansion and attended by mink attired mannequins in the latest Paris fashions.

Recently the Israeli delegation to one of the innumerable conferences held in Europe under U.N. auspices debated among themselves the question of whether they really belonged at the meeting, since its theme was "Growth in Underdeveloped Nations." Perhaps if the delegates left Tel Aviv or Haifa and wandered among the smaller towns they would not ask that question.

Israel has made enormous strides; it still has an enormous way to go. Putting eighteenth-century people in twentieth-century buildings is no answer. What is the answer? The army is one; it does an outstanding job of acculturation. The others are time, patience, faith, and the Income Tax Department, all of which are elements in the synthesis of the civilization that is and will be Israel. Until then, the diversity is marvelous, unless you're the type who doesn't like to take milk from babies when going to the hardware store.

There is an Arab café in Jaffa which, according to popular legend, is owned and operated by an "Arab" from Warsaw. There are, however, many, many genuine Arab eating places in Israel. One in particular that I often frequent is in Ramle.

The café in Ramle is operated by the Israeli Arab version of the Marx Brothers. They are however, a slightly less distinguished-looking crew, since their moustaches haven't as yet grown to full glory. Their father, who was presumably the founder of the place, stares down benignly from his picture on the wall, looking for all the world like an overweight Nasser.

The service is atrocious, mainly because one brother does the cooking, one the waiting on tables, and one goofs off in the yard fixing his car. Instead of sitting down at the table when you enter, you first go into the kitchen and demand your meal. *Menus?* Why waste the paper? You then sit down, only to get up at least twice before something appears on the table.

What appears is good, even excellent if you've got the lead-lined guts to eat hot pickled eggplant (delicious) and pickled peppers. The Arab bread, or *pita*, is wonderful when fresh. It resembles two 7-inch paper plates glued together around the rims with the doughy part forming a pouch inside. With it you can scoop, eat, scrape, and store food with the utmost of grace and simplicity.

After wallowing through the salad, you can give your stomach a rest by eying the other patrons. There is usually at least one table of genuine robe-clad Arabs eating, smoking, and talking in shifts. These boys, mostly sheep and goat herders, are really a fierce-looking lot with scowling, deeply furrowed faces and wild eyes. Looks however are deceiving, because at that time they were a pretty peaceful bunch, counting their profits or their prayer beads.

The rest of the café looks like a mess hall of the Israeli

Army. Anyway, it always has its quota of NCO's of both sexes. The place is relatively clean by Israeli standards. Frankly, outside of the hotels, a spic and span eatery in Israel is rare indeed. Howard Johnson could make a killing here.

The Arab restaurants are really mobbed during Passover. The bread hungry crowds rise out of Tel Aviv and descend on these humble places like an eleventh plague. Israel is unique in the number of its citizens who will go to any lengths to violate the Law rather than fulfill it, and what better place than a *pita* palace on Passover.

ANTS

———◆———

When I lived in America, I had a mania for book clubs. I'd join any old club and take anything available just to fill my shelves. Among the gems I got on one occasion was a thick volume, *Thirty Stories to Remember*. It lay idle in TV America for many months.

Here in TV-less Israel the book was undusted, and I discovered, much to my surprise, some of the best reading of the decade. One of the stories, "Leiningen Versus the Ants," stands out in my mind. It tells of the almost unsuccessful attempt of an English planter in Brazil's Amazon jungle to battle off annihilation by an army of ants.

Things are not that bad in Israel — yet. The really threatening armies locally are Arab, but the ants do wage incessant guerrilla warfare on the populace.

In Cleveland we had only two kinds of ants, little and big. In Israel we have big, bigger, biggest, plusbig, and superbig. The little one's have long since died out, in adherence to Darwinism.

The average Israeli ant is about as hard to describe as the average Israeli, but his general characteristics are: black, hungry, and everywhere. They get into the pots, the pans, the dishes, the cereal, the sugar, the tea, and on the sabbath, the sacramental wine. They have great respect for property. They consider it all to be their own and busily transfer bits of it in every direction. If you should forget to dump your garbage one night and leave it on the back stoop, no worry, it will be picked clean by morning.

There is one species that seems to be particularly at home here. It is a little over 20 millimeters (that's about ¾ inch) long and the posterior projects upward at about a 40 degree angle from the ground. As it tears around helter-skelter with its companions it conveys the impression of Ditzengoff Square.

VIEWS ON VIEWS

I have a friend in Israel who lives in a very mundane house with a very magnificent view. Actually, for a Midwesterner, most any view in Israel is spectacular. But there is something special about the view from Arieh's house. Although Arieh lives only a block away from us, the difference in views is fantastic.

From our rear terrace we have a view that slopes lovingly over orange groves, flits by the abandoned Minaret of Yehudia, an ex-Arab town that once sheltered the original founders of Petach Tikvah, and then climbs gracefully but steadily through the foothills of Judea. It does not stop for the unnatural border which separates Israel from Jordan here, but continues to climb mountain peaks as aged as time until it disappears in the mists above Ramallah. On clear days, and even more so on the many crystal clear nights, it's possible, although some of my neighbors will argue this, to see the lights of Jerusalem, 20 miles away.

Arieh has this view and much more. If we look out of the windows facing east in our home we see the typical but unlovely visage of the new home going up next door. Everyone in Israel lives next to something going up next door, so perhaps we cannot complain. Sitting on a chair on the front lawn of Arieh's home, however, one can see to the east the sand dunes near Holon and the sea beyond, and to the west the entire panorama of the Judean foothills. When Arieh says he is looking across Israel, he is doing just that.

Strangely enough, this very compactness, instead of giving one a feeling of uneasiness, gives one a feeling of serenity. I have always felt that asking God to watch over the United States was a pretty tough task. Surely watching over this little land, which even the human eye can encompass, shouldn't be too great a burden.

WANTED: A GOOD GEVES MAN

Among the stock of useless information I have acquired in my lifetime is the fact that the word "gypsum" is derived, like the word "gypsies," from our dear neighbor to the south, Egypt. Most of my life I couldn't have cared less, but, since living in Israel, I have become keenly aware of them both, Egypt and gypsum.

First, let me state categorically that there is no such thing as a crack-free wall in Israel. The reason, builders will tell you, is that the walls are settling. Of course, some walls have been settling for fifty years, but no matter: if you have a crack, there is always *geves* (gypsum).

The impatience of the Israeli population I know about, but impatient chemicals, this I never heard of. When I bought my first *geves* at the local hardware store, the owner warned me, "Only mix a little at a time. It gets hard on you."

I soon learned the wisdom of his words. I am not a neophyte plasterer, having done some miserable simple repairs in America, but never had I encountered anything like *geves*. When I got the stuff home, I mixed a little in (I was going to say old, but no glass jar in Israel is ever old) a glass jar, set it down, yelled at my wife (traditional during repair work), chipped the loose plaster from the hole, and grabbed the stick to apply the plaster.

Not only did I get the mixing stick, but I also got the jar and the plaster in one lovely solidified lump. Since I have an innate horror of time study experts, I have never put a stopwatch on *geves* to determine its rate of hardening. But I feel it's safe to say that if you don't apply it in three minutes you're lost.

So many Israelis have been lost, in fact, that a national artifact known as the "*geves* bowl" has come into being. A *geves* bowl is nothing but a cereal bowl made of soft rubber. The closest thing to it in America usually has a handle on it and is used to unclog toilets. No instructions come with geves bowls, so

103

in order to facilitate integration for future Western immigrants, I would like to outline a few.

1) Grip *geves* bowl firmly.
2) Pour in *geves.*
3) Add water and mix.
4) Apply *geves* to wall. Ninety per cent of the *geves* has now hardened to the walls of the *geves* bowl.
5) Crunch *geves* bowl and crack off hard *geves.* Repeat again and again and again.
6) Give the whole thing up and call a *geves* man.

The only trouble with step six is that there are no good *geves* men in Israel, just a bunch of rank amateurs. Every electrician, carpenter, plumber, clerk, and customs clearer considers himself a *geves* man, and the walls of many a home and factory are full of mute evidence of their dismal failures. Eternally preserved fingerprints, thumbprints, knuckleprints, and even an occasional fistprint proclaim the *geves* man's disgust.

There are two ways out of the *geves* dilemma: Bring along some plaster of Paris from America, which is ridiculous, or build a crack-free home, which is impossible. I guess the *geves* bowl is here to stay.

HAMANIA

One of the football songs of the predominantly Jewish high school I attended went something like this:

Abie, Ikie, Moe and Sam
We're the boys that don't eat ham
Grab your matzos, hold them tight
Come on Glenville, fight, fight, fight.

This ditty would be untrue of for any Israeli sports team unless perhaps the second line was changed to "We're the boys that always crave ham," for the secular Israeli public has a ham fixation that is astonishing. It's also a little embarrassing, and statistics on ham consumption or pig breeding are noticeably absent from any foreign-oriented Israeli publications.

My first encounter with this obsession was on a visit to an avant-garde Israeli-Italian restaurant with a many-generationed-sabra Israeli couple. As an entrée the waiter suggested, "Perhaps a little ham and cheese?" Now I have eaten in hundreds of American restaurants and never in any one of them has any waiter suggested ham and cheese as an entrée or has this delicacy ever even appeared on the menu. Next to offering baby calf boiled in its mother's milk, I don't think this restaurant could have picked a better combination to violate the Dietary Laws and my amazement at the time was quite profound.

I was not amazed for long, however, for I soon found out that hamania was an integral part of the Israeli scene.

Item: The six passengers on the almost empty El Al flight I am on are bounced off the plane in London and transferred to BOAC for the flight to New York. During the brief stopover, the Americans and Europeans order tea, coffee, cookies, etc., at the luncheon counter; the lone Israeli, a ham sandwich.

Item: The busiest restaurant in Lydda is a greasy spoon with a well larded specialty, ham sandwiches.

Item: A group of observant immigrants from India are settled by the Jewish Agency in a leftist kibbutz in the Galilee. Their first meal in the holy land — ham.

Why this ham fixation? A manifestation of the complete break of the Israeli present with the Jewish Diaspora past? A revolt against the religious regulations of Israeli public life? A craving for the forbidden as part of the general Israeli *chutzpa* syndrome? Or do they just plain like ham? Who knows? And what difference does it make? The Israeli public will continue to ham it up.

BLOCKIM

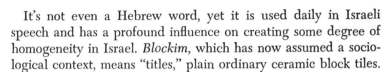

It's not even a Hebrew word, yet it is used daily in Israeli speech and has a profound influence on creating some degree of homogeneity in Israel. *Blockim*, which has now assumed a sociological context, means "titles," plain ordinary ceramic block tiles. Practically every household, from the newly arrived immigrant's flat in Eilat to the palatial summer home of the president of the Bank of Israel, is covered with the same size, same color, and same style, ceramic tile. About the only difference between households is how the tile is laid. Normally, a base of fine sand is spread on the earth, upon which a layer of cement one-half to one inch thick is spread just before a tile is set in place. The thickness of the base, the type and thickness of cement, and the knowledge of the workman are what determines whether a tile floor remains level or becomes a depressed checkerboard.

One of the most interesting excuses Israelis find for taking a vacation is having their sunken floors replaced. The entire house has to be torn up and usually the premises are vacated by the family for the month's time needed to complete the average job.

Years ago Arab and Israeli houses had beautiful floral designs and patterns laid in their floors, giving each home a distinctive appearance. When the architectural revolution which dictated only one style of tile occurred, I haven't been able to ascertain. Perhaps some giant Histadrut enterprise swallowed up all the competition and dictated that henceforth all floors would be socialist brown with marbleized chips.

One of the nice things about this color is that the sand that covers every Israeli household blends in nicely with the tiles. Actually, aside from the crunching sounds when you walk, it's sometimes very difficult to tell whether the floor is clean or not.

I first learned about the social import of *blockim* when I overheard a conversation:

107

"How big is your kitchen?"

"About fourteen by twenty-three, with a laundry room eight by nine. How big is yours?"

"I think its about twelve by twenty-two."

I finally broke down and asked the two women who had been speaking about their kitchens in our Ulpan what they meant by fourteen by twenty-three — feet? meters? an obscure South African measure?

"What do you mean, what fourteen by twenty-three? *Blockim* of course."

"You mean you measure that way?"

"Of course, don't you?"

"No."

"You will, you will."

"*Pheh*," I thought. "Never."

Then the day came when we went house hunting. Would our refrigerator fit in the kitchen? How about the kids' beds against this wall? No need to measure, just use the built-in Israeli graph paper. For the purists the normal block is 20 centimeters, or 5 blocks per meter.

Israel is the only country in the world where when kids want to compare heights they don't stand up against a wall, they lay down on the floor.

GREETINGS

I suppose when you stop to think about it, probably many of the first Christmas carols were written by Jews. Their descendents have carried on in this tradition, at least in the U.S.A. A good friend of mine who works in one of the largest greeting card companies in America, spends a good two to three months of the year writing Christmas cards; or maybe it was designing — come to think of it, there's not an awful lot you can say on a Christmas card.

Be this as it may, the Jews have played a significant part in flooding the American public with greetings for every occasion. Their co-religionists in Israel have done a miserable job by comparison.

The Hanukkah card, which is a big counter-Christmas thing in America, is practically nonexistent in Israel, where, frankly, who needs it? The one item that is significant is the Rosh Hashanah, or New Year's card. In the first few weeks of September, the principal corners of all the large thoroughfares in the cities begin to sprout, in addition to assorted beggars, felafel stands, and flies, small New Year's greeting card stands.

The quality of their offering is, in the main, atrocious. Some of the cheesiest, crummiest, tinseliest designs the twisted artistic mind can conceive are offered as vehicles for New Year's greeting. For a country with such a plethora of artists, one would think that a few would be willing to lend their talents to the greeting card industry.

We've received many New Year's cards in Israel after our first year here and certainly it is the wish not the vehicle which conveys the feeling. However, I must confess that the most beautiful card we received says on the back: "A Forget*Me*Not Card, Cape & Transvaal Printers Ltd., South Africa."

One wonders how many years we can continue to receive cards from west of Down Under.

CURRENCY AESTHETICS

There is something solid-looking about a dollar bill. The black Gothic frame, the steely eyes of George Washington, and the eye on the back staring at you — all seem to say: "This paper is worth a buck" — or was.

Israeli currency does not demand this respect. Frankly, I still keep thinking it's Monopoly money.

As a reaction to the millenniums of restriction on art for religious reasons, Israel today has an abundance of artists. They certainly went wild when they designed the latest batch of Israeli currency.

The blue one-pound note has a fisherman on it who looks like he came right out of Gloucester Bay. Granted he has a beard, but he looks more from Moby Dick than from Moshe. He's weighed down with enough paraphernalia to sink any boat he steps into.

In keeping with a monetary tradition, the front side (English reverse) of the pound note has a replica of an ancient synagogue mosaic. Quite nice, quite dignified.

Next to this mosaic, however, is the peephole, which disfigures all the Israeli currency, an elliptical area about two inches high completely white and bare. Ah, but hold it to the light and what do we see? An enlarged head of our fisherman friend glowing in all his watermarked glory.

The other bills are just as garrish, with one respectable archeological side and one twentieth-century nightmare. The previous issue of currency had more dignity in the opinion of many Israelis. For a country that has done such a magnificent job on designing aesthetically beautiful postage stamps, one would expect more from the currency.

Meanwhile, aesthetic, aeshmetic, I'll still keep collecting the stuff. It comes in awful handy in fulfilling non-artistic wants.

WHAT MAKES SAMMY RUN IN ISRAEL?

One of the legendary assets Jews have developed in the Diaspora is a sense of salesmanship. The Jewish peddler and his twentieth-century counterpart, the Jewish salesman, have become an integral part of the past and present American scene. Jewish salesmanship, both in fiction and in fact, has played a vital part in the rapid rise of the American Jewish community from rags to riches.

How has this salesmanship attitude grown, nurtured, and developed in Israel? What is the attitude of the typical Israeli salesman or salesperson? Let me describe it in four words I have heard many times since my residence here: "I couldn't care less."

Go into practically any one of the hundreds and hundreds of small shops lining a main street in Tel Aviv, browse around, pick up an item. Will anyone ask you if you need help? Will the owner, his wife, or his mother-in-law inquire whether they can serve you by reducing your cash balance? No, they will not. You will be completely ignored, snubbed, and in extreme cases even rebuked.

Countless times, I have stood gazing into store windows on Allenby Road in Tel Aviv. One word of encouragement from the owner, who usually lolls in the entrance, would have turned me from a gazer into a buyer. It never came. As far as the average Israeli storekeeper is concerned, the customer does not exist until he makes himself known by asking a question or appealing for permission to purchase something.

Adequate advertising, customer and public relations are in the neophyte stage in Israel. Sammy doesn't run in Israel. He just stands there and doesn't give a damn. Who knows? Maybe it's better that way.

THE BANANA REPUBLIC

Somehow you just don't think of Israel as being a "banana republic." Bananas come from Central America, period. With the vast Israeli interest and emphasis on agriculture, practically every crop in the world has been planted here experimentally during the past fifty years and bananas are one crop that has thrived and provided Israel with additional export dollars.

Bananas are really not new to Palestine. At the turn of the century there were isolated banana groves in the Jericho oasis and a venturesome Sephardi merchant brought some to Jerusalem for sale to an unreceptive public. They never did catch on, and until the past decade or so, bananas were not a staple in the Israeli diet.

Banana plantations were first planted by the *kibbutzim* and *moshavim* in the Jordan Valley, where the winters are hot and water is relatively plentiful. I don't know what the first crops were like, but four years ago on my first visit to Israel, the average banana looked like an overgrown pinky. Today, bananas have developed into something resembling the standard American product, although they are still smaller in size.

Banana plantations have spread to many areas of the country and the traveler on the Haifa-Tel Aviv train gets a quick glimpse of bananaland.

In about three years I hope to be an expert on bananas, since I've planted three trees in my garden. Until that time, here is the minimal advice I can offer the non-banana-growing Jewish public.

Banana leaves may be good for trays at Hawaiian luaus but they're no good for roofing a succah. The enormous leaves shrivel overnight when cut and make a limp mess on the succah roof.

There is some controversy over the religio-botanical nature

of bananas: whether the blessing on them for fruit of the earth or fruit of the trees is appropriate. If in doubt, say both.

One of my earliest recollections about bananas was that a creepy, hairy tarantula at least six inches in diameter was to be found on every sixth stalk. This they have as yet not found in Israel, but they will. *Yesh hakol be' Eretz.* "There is everything in Israel."

EXTENSION CORD LIVING

The Hebrew word for electricity is taken from a biblical phrase which describes the sparkling or sparking appearance of the angels surrounding God's throne. The people who produce and manage the supply of electricity in Israel are no angels, but they have surrounded themselves with a throne of profit and plenty that makes the Israel Electric Company one of the most formidable operations in the country.

It's true that even in America you can't buy electricity from whomever you please, but at least the country is large enough to support some competition in the field, which is not the case in Israel.

All of Israel's electricity is made from oil, 90 per cent of which is imported. Consequently it's expensive, unless you happen to be an employee of the Electric Company. As part of the socialist endeavors which own and operate a good part of Israel, the Histadrut workers in the Israel Electric Company share in the company by getting electric power at greatly reduced rates, which seems a rather unjust situation.

If you come to one of the vast *shikunim,* or housing developments, where the bulk of Israel's population lives, chances are one apartment in the building will be glowing like, you should pardon the expression, a Christmas tree. Most people in Israel have gas stoves and flourescent outdoor lights. They're cheaper to operate. In this apartment, however, you're sure to find an electric stove, regular light bulbs, and even an array of electric room heaters. These boys are living electrically to the hilt.

Most people in Israel cannot live on their salaries. Moonlighting is second nature to a good portion of the population. This being the case, I often wondered why the electrical company employees don't go in for extension cord living. One or two cords dangling down into neighbors' apartments could make a nice living for the enterprising entrepreneur. But, alas, such free enterprise is frowned on by governmental authorities. Well, you can always marry into the company.

TEST

Once a year, whether he likes it or not, every motorist in Israel has to face up to the terrifying ordeal known as *test* in Hebrew. It bears a striking resemblance to the English word and denotes the annual inspection that every motor vehicle in the country must go through.

Not that it clears the road of wrecks. There are more wretched-looking junkyard candidates on Israeli roads than the average American sees in a lifetime. Then they must all have good steering, good wheel alignment, proper lights and brakes, right? No, wrong. When driving at night in Israel you can be assured that the lights of 50 percent of the oncoming vehicles are beamed at one place, your face.

Test has brought with it an original Israeli phenomenon, *pre-test, test.* Thus a typical motorist drives down to the central testing station a Holon, a suburb of Tel Aviv, but before joining the five-block lineup, he turns off the road and enters a private garage. Here he gets wheels aligned, lights checked and, for a fee, a tester will take his car through the test. Having an innate dislike of bureaucracy, I chose to take this easy way out.

After turning over all my documents to the tester, I stood there passportless, carless, anxiously watching my tester's progress through the queue. Through his good personal *protectzia,* he got through the first checkpoint only about ten minutes later than it would have taken me had I done the job myself, and then disappeared into the labyrinth of hanger-like brake, light, and steering test sections.

He finally reappeared only an hour and a half after his scheduled return with the happy news that my car suffered from a slack steering wheel, a condition that could be corrected immediately in two or three hours.

Abandoning all hope of retrieving my car that day, I released it into the loving hands of the chisel wielding mechanics who were busy prying at its innards, and hitchhiked home in the rain.

That night two unknown figures greeted me at my doorstep, the number one tester and his special assistant. They needed my insurance papers, which I had proffered to them but which they had refused that morning.

Last year it took me four days to get my car back from *test*, during which time I'm certain it saw *sherut* ("bus") service on the Tel Aviv-Eilat run. This year perhaps I'll be luckier and get it back with just a mere 200 kilometer jaunt to Tiberias registered on it.

TO MARKET, TO MARKET

One of the prescribed rites for tourists in Israel is to get up at five o'clock Thursday morning and be dragged down to Beersheva to see the Bedouin market. They needn't bother; they can see just as much filth and frolic by going to Lydda on Tuesday morning. The only item Lydda can't compete with Beersheva on is camels, so if you're a connoisseur, head south.

Although it doesn't have camels, Lydda has sheep, goats, cows, horses, turkeys, chickens, geese, and people. People — all kinds, colors, and classes. The tall gaunt pitch-black Negro Bedouins stand out like latter day Abrahams in their *keffiahs* and flowing robes. Others, like the hordes of Morrocan and Algerian women in their overprinted sacklike dresses, blend into the multichromatic background.

The Indian women are striking with their carefully groomed coiffures, their immaculate saris, their quiet speech, and still remarkable for Israel, good manners. They add an air of the exotic Far, to the already colorful, Near East.

Sprinkled here and there in the crowd are the *chatichot,* the "pieces," Israel's twentieth-century women with beehive hairdos and beautiful dresses at least two inches too short and three sizes too tight, which travel to fascinating levels whenever they stoop to examine produce.

The Yemenite women are here, too, with their sexless sheaths and ankle-length variegated trousers underneath. Their men, with their wizened, prophetic looks, their scraggly beards, and earlocks, are much more colorful characters.

There is order here, and there is chaos. Thankfully most of the horses are left across the street to graze, leaving occasional goat and sheep droppings, chicken feathers, wilted vegetables, and blood as the only obstacles to navigation.

There are a few temporary stalls, but most of the produce and plastic items are scattered on the ground with the owners perched in their midst. Being basically an agricultural market, vegetables and fruits predominate. Most of the items are grown by the sellers in the surrounding farms and are an excellent example of comparative agriculture. Lovely, large, crisp potatoes from one farm compete easily with undersized, shriveled specimens from his neighbor. Apples that would be at home in the A & P lie side by side with those fit only for hog fodder.

The abundance is lovely to behold. There are mountains of garlic, which saturate the air with pungent odor. Huge squashes, an Israeli staple, burst out of their containers and sprawl on the ground. Plump, solid chickens, sitting in stupid, uncomprehending silence or squawking hideously in awareness of their fate, fill a corner of the market to overflowing. The only items which are lacking are milk and honey.

Cows change hands; goats are bartered; sheep priced, pinched, and slaughtered; and the only real loser in a day's business is the Israeli Income Tax Department, which cannot possibly keep track of the tin-can and back-pocket accounts most of the farmers keep.

There is an aisle of clothing — dresses, shirts, and shoes. Shoddy material poorly sewn, ill-fitting and high-priced. For the wives who sew, there is an assortment of hideous fabrics. There are pots and pans and dishes and strainers and *pita* vendors and ice cream vendors, olive oil sellers, nut vendors, spice vendors, but, alas, no book vendors. A kaleidoscope of color, a cacophony of sound, picturesque to the Western eye, prosaic everyday life to the Israeli.

LEAPIN' LIZARDS

Since I settled in Israel I have become a reptile-watcher. There are no lizards (four-footed ones, that is) in Tel Aviv. It's too civilized for that now. But I remember spotting, in the living room of friends in Tzahala, a suburb of Tel Aviv, a six-inch chameleon slink across the wall. A shriek went up from another guest: "How can you stand those in your house?" "Oh, they don't bother us. It's bad luck to kill them."

Also, it's practically impossible. There is nothing as fleet-footed as an Israeli lizard. The closest study I've ever been able to make was of a twitching salamander's tail, which remained on our child's bedroom floor after I had gingerly dispatched the rest of it out the window.

The average lizard, like the average Israeli, is rather small but ferocious, and is in a big hurry to do nothing. It will slither maniacally across a tile roof then stop for a half-hour siesta in the sun.

For certain tribes in the southern Philippines, lizard meat is a great delicacy. Alas, lizards are not kosher. Even if they were, what ritual slaughterer would want to qualify in lizards? *Pheh!*

OURS OR THEIRS?

It used to be the tallest building in Jerusalem until Hechal Shlomo, the Chief Rabbinate building was built a few years ago. Still, the Jerusalem Y.M.C.A. Building is an impressive sight. James Newbegin Jarvil, a pre-U.J.A. philanthropist, built it in 1928 and through the years it has housed Moslem, Christian, and Jew in varying states of harmony.

The view from the tower is magnificent. On a clear day you can see across the Jordanian-occupied area of Palestine to the Dead Sea and the blue-grey mountains of Moab beyond. Here Moses stood and looked longingly into the land to which God had so laboriously brought his people: "Get thee up into this mountain — and behold the land of Canaan, which I give unto the children of Israel for a possession."

This day one of God's youngest children was looking back at Moses' mountain. A typical Israeli boy, he wore blue pants that were too short, and had sturdy, bronzed legs, black curly hair, and the smile and curiosity of a seven-year-old. His father was showing him the sights of Jerusalem.

They were looking westward when we reached the observation platform. The boy babbled in the stark staccato of Israeli Hebrew. He probably was pointing out friends' homes or familiar sights; we were not linguists enough at the time to tell.

Then they went to the eastern side, and we caught a phrase that still lingers today — "Shel lachem o shelanu?" "Ours or theirs?" Over and over again the boy pointed to various sites — the original Hebrew University, the Temple area, the Mount of Olives — ours or theirs?

Perhaps when this little boy becomes a man in Israel he will not have to answer such questions for his son.

IV

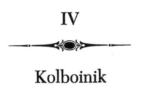

Kolboinik

TOP SECRET

In a country with so many enemies and so little space, secrecy is a full-time job. I think most of the intrigue was invented as a crutch for tourist guides, because when a guide can't identify a site he covers up by claiming it's a "military object." The country, is strewn with military objects and there are hundreds of jokes concerning them. My favorite story, however, is not a joke but fact.

After graduating from the Technion as a top-notch metallurgical engineer, my friend Allon applied for a job in Military Industries Plant No. 15. After an exchange of letters and an interview at Haifa Army Headquarters, he received a letter confirming his employment and was ordered to report for work the following Sunday morning.

Just one little problem. In keeping with military secrecy, no return address was on the letter and no one had told him where Plant No. 15 was.

So he just took the letter and went down to Headquarters and asked the desk clerk: "Could you please tell me how to get to Military Industries Plant No. 15?"

"What do you want to know for?"

"I'm supposed to start work there this morning. Here, here's a letter telling me to report to work."

"Sorry, Plant No. 15 is a military object. We're not allowed to reveal its location."

"But I'm supposed to be working there."

"Sorry."

Allon then proceeded to the office of the Staff Sergeant for the Northern Army Command. He got the same answer.

Somehow he managed to wangle his way into the Office of the Assistant Commander for the Northern Military District. Did it help? Like a hole in the head. "Plant No. 15 is a military object and cannot be revealed to unauthorized personnel."

Well, Allon, drawing on his many years of experience in the country, suddenly got a brainstorm.

He left the Army offices in disgust and walked over to the nearest taxi stand, got in and told the driver: "Take me to Military Industries Plant No. 15."

He was there in twenty minutes.

EVERY MAN HIS PRIVATE

The last time I heard an American talking about his "private," he was a rather fastidious fellow, trying, unsuccessfully, to use clean words to tell a dirty joke. In Israel the "private" also refers to a unique and precious piece of equipment, one's own automobile.

It is the fervent desire and hope of every Israeli youth to fulfill his non-Zionist dream of someday having a private of his own. Sadly, it is just a dream to most because the price of cars is astronomical. One of the American low-priced three, which would sell in the States for $3,000, would cost approximately three times as much in Israel, or I £ 27,000. Shipping costs are nominal: the average car costs $300 to $400 to ship from the States and substantially less from Italy or France. What makes the price tag so high are customs duties and purchase tax, which double and triple the value of the car, until a Volkswagon becomes a luxury even for the well-to-do. For many years this policy succeeded in keeping Israel relatively auto-free. Its effectiveness was brought home to me when I asked a sabra the reason a lovely beach between Tel Aviv and Ashdod is shown as the Diplomats Beach on the map. He explained that no buses ran out there, and up to five or six years ago, the only people who could frequent the place in any numbers were diplomats with their own transportation.

Things have changed, and despite customs duties, port clearance fees, defense stamp taxes, license fees, and the general cussedness of the average car salesman, Israel is beginning to be swamped with vehicles of every size and description. People are selling homes, land, and occasionally wives (among our Bedouin brethren) in order to buy cars. Dealer garages and wreckers are mushrooming in a growing crescendo of steel, rubber, and panel banging. Who knows where it will end. In the next election some fringe party is sure to capture the Knesset. All they need is the slogan: "Every man a prince with his private!"

WATCHING THE WORLD GO BY

One of the most energetically pursued Israeli occupations is sitting, just sitting, anyplace and anywhere. The Middle-European café sitters, the Levantine siesta sitters, and the Arabic squatters have blended together in Israel to establish a national pastime — sitting, sipping, and staring.

Chair-making must be a highly profitable occupation in Israel. There are probably as many chairs as people in a (I was going to say square, but no blocks in Israel are square) block, in Tel Aviv's commercial district. Café seats, for which one is obligated to buy at least one cup of coffee every four or five hours to justify his tenancy, are plentiful, but strategically placed park benches are far too few and are highly prized.

On a sunny winter morning my wife, who is in a better position to verify these statistics, made the following observations while waiting for me on a Tel Aviv park bench.

First, and most obvious, was the bedraggled North African immigrant sitting, smiling, and singing beautifully at the top of his voice. The consensus of opinion of passersby were (1) that he was slightly *meshuga*, or (2) that he was slightly inebriated. The flask he withdrew periodically from his inner pocket indicated that the latter was correct.

Directly next to the crocked Caruso sat the perennial student, bearded, bespectacled, and engrossed in a revolutionary paperback. He was completely oblivious to the arias surrounding him.

Next to my wife sat an old German lady, watching her every knit and pearl, her years full, her time free. Happily, hers was a generation that came to Israel to live, not to die, as so many elderly people had come in the past.

Then there were the men-about-town, or anything else there is to be about. After a few multilingual questions concerning my wife's marital status and ascertaining that someone was meeting her in fifteen minutes, their interest waned.

Israelis are their own best audience and in this diverse society sitting and staring is a worthwhile occupation.

There is only one motoring experience more terrifying to the foreign driver than driving through Israeli traffic by day, and that is driving by night. One of the cardinal rules of the Israeli cyclist or pedestrian is, "If they can't see me, they can't hit me."

Imagine the appalling sensation when, motoring at 50 miles per hour on a pitch-black country road, you suddenly find four reflectorless bicycles materializing in your path. You can jam on your brakes, but then the ever present sand or cement truck breathing down your neck is sure to park in your front seat.

What do you do? You curse, or you pray, as your conscience guides you but just as you expect to hear the sound of splintering spokes, the phantom foursome will peel off the road to reappear for the next line of cars.

Even worse than bicycles are hitchhiking soldiers who materialize suddenly from the inky roadside blackness and prostrate themselves in front of your oncoming auto. The casualty rate here far outstrips that in the border clashes.

Two years ago, the government took a step to reduce nighttime collisions by ordering all car owners to purchase red tape and triangles. Coming from a government that is built on red tape, this seemed a logical move to most citizens, and miles of reflective red stickum tape were sold to motorists, much to the delight of the 3M representative.

This was one red tape regulation, however, which has really paid off. All the cars, wagons, buses, scooters, and tractors in the country now have red reflective tape on their butts, and rear-end collisions at night have gone down to nil. There is a special red reflective triangle that is carried and set out on the road when a motorist is changing a tire. These are two procedures that the U.S. would do well to emulate.

I wonder when 3M will come up with a tape that will stick to a camel.

GETTING INTO HOT WATER

One of the most difficult things to do in Israel is to get into hot water. With no central gas supply and very little central heating in the country, there are two classic ways of heating water, by solar water heaters and by electricity.

Solar heaters are practically a trademark of the country, and every *shikun* (typical Israeli "apartment house") roof seems to have forests of them. The exposing chambers, in which the water is heated, are inconspicuous window-like fixtures angled to receive the maximum sun. The water storage tanks, however, are quite prominent, piercing the sky like giant thumbs.

Although sunshine is one of the few things people do not pay for in this country, there are drawbacks to the sun heaters. In winter when the need is most acute that lucky ole sun, despite the travel agent's ads, doesn't always shine.

Like most of our neighbors here, we've got a special-plan electric water heater. The special plan, I think, is that the electric company believes you should only take one hot bath or shower per week. The heaters operate on a different circuit from the regular electrical supply and have their own meter and time clock. They switch on at about ten o'clock at night, which is great for giving the kiddies midnight showers.

What hot water is produced during the night is usually adequate only for dish- and clothes-washing, so you really have to be a logistician to plan your baths. One of our neighbors gets up regularly at 2:00 A.M. to luxuriate in a hot shower.

The mere existence of hot water is a luxury in Israel. There are countless *shikunim* where such facilities are nonexistent. Bathtubs too are not standard Israeli fare, and to many Western immigrants in development towns, nostalgia for this fundamental fixture makes adaptation difficult.

Of course, in the summer, Israelis have a simple solution to the bathing problem: the 83° Mediterranean and the even warmer Galilee and Dead seas are only a hitchhike away.

MADE IN ISRAEL

In Israel anything you buy is divided into two categories *Totzeret Aretz* ("Product of the Land," i.e. made in Israel) and *Totzeret Chutz* (made anyplace else). *Totzeret Chutz* is better.

It is really astonishing that a people who take such fierce national pride in their freedom, in their army, in their redemption of the land should have so little pride in their industrial products. Perhaps this is because, up to very recently, there wasn't very much to have pride in. Israel produced light bulbs that froze stuck in sockets, electrical plugs that pulled apart after a week's use, and bathroom fixtures on which the plating peeled in sheets.

But things are changing. In competing for an export market that demands quality, Israel has begun to produce many quality items for her own consumption. Since the best of everything — wine, citrus fruits, and clothing — is sent abroad, the word "export," chanted by sidewalk hawkers has become synonymous with quality to the Israeli buyer.

The industrial market, too, is beginning to place some faith in Israeli products, particularly small machine tool bits, drills, cutters, and presses. When the local mechanics begin to fill their toolboxes with Israeli made tools, you'll know that the market has arrived.

Because of Israel's unique geographic position, local importers can bring in goods from England, Western Europe, America, and Japan with almost equal ease. Thus if the imports are eased on a particular item, the Israeli manufacturer must compete with the best that the free world, and sometimes not-so-free world, can offer. Putting Israeli products up against this type of competition can have only beneficial results quality-wise, but the economic effects are a subject of constant governmental and industry bickering.

An Israeli acquaintance of ours found herself in New York one rainy fall and went shopping in one of the larger department stores for a raincoat. She was shown a number of smart American- and English-made coats and then the saleslady brought out their pièce-de-résistance — a lovely coat made in Israel, which she could have bought for 30 per cent less in any shop in Ditzengoff. Perhaps a product is without honor in its own country.

HARBINGER OF SPRING

For the Israeli, spring begins at the end of February or the beginning of March. For an American from the northern climes, it seems as if spring has never quite left Israel, since throughout the winter, with all its rain, wind, and cold, there are always flowers blooming and the landscape is a verdant, if sometimes soggy, green.

The official harbinger of spring in Israel is the *shkadiah*, or almond tree. Because of Israel's unusual climate, it is a common sight to see, side by side, large orchards of citrus trees, and fruit- and nut-bearing trees such as the peach, pear, almond, and apple. The citrus trees are in their glory during the winter months, their branches drooping with a profusion of gigantic oranges, grapefruits, and lemons, while alongside them sit the deciduous fruit trees bare, naked, and shivering from the cold.

Just about the time the last picker has finally plucked the last stray orange from the orchard, the almond trees begin to perk up. Sometime at the end of February, they burst forth in a beautiful array of pinkish-white blossoms. As the almond blossoms begin to fade, peach, pear, apple, and quince blossoms rebirth, and as the fruit trees start to yield, their ranks are the days grow hotter, the oranges once again begin their cycle of rebirth and, as the fruit trees start to yield, their ranks are filled by countless fragrant orange blossoms that perfume the country air for miles around.

From the first almond bud to the last orange blossom, spring in Israel is a delight for the eye, a sweet savor for the nose, and a warm place in the heart.

SAVE YOUR CZARIST BONDS

About a hundred years ago, it was the up-and-coming thing for European power to acquire territory in the Holy Land and to establish hospices or monasteries to house their pilgrims. Among the most zealous countries was Russia, and the Russian Orthodox Church purchased some choice sites in Jerusalem, Jaffa, and elsewhere.

The Russian Compound in Jerusalem won a certain fame by being part of a security zone for government offices during the British Mandatory period. It was surrounded by multiple rows of barbed-wire fencing and was constantly patroled by British soldiers. The fortress-like appearance earned it the name of Bevingrad, after Ernest Bevin, who was the English anti-Israel Foreign Secretary.

With statehood, Israel became the custodian, landlord, and guardian of a number of properties that were to give it untold legalistic headaches in the ensuing years. Among these were the former Russian Czarist possessions, now claimed by Soviet Russia. For fifteen years there has been a quiet international wrangle between Israel and the Soviet Union on who owes whom, how much, and for what.

Although Russia vied with the United States as to who would be the first to recognize Israel, the initial bloom of friendship quickly melted and practically vaporized completely after Israel's Sinai Campaign in 1956. At that time Israel again became the custodian of millions of dollars worth of Russian property, including tanks, guns, and arms sent by Russia to Egypt for implementing Israel's destruction.

The Russians were never particularly anxious to claim kinship to the arms Israel's army captured, but they still held a fond attachment to their old Czarist property. Suddenly, in early 1964, a surprising settlement was reached. Israel would pay Russia I£ 4.5 million (about $1.5 million) for the property, with almost half of the payment in Israeli goods. This was hailed in many circles as the beginning of a thaw in Moscow-Jerusalem relations, although many thought it a rather expensive thaw.

One wonders if precedents of this kind will someday prod Russia into the other side of the fence and promote the payment of the Czarist bonds that have been floating in and out of securities circles for almost a generation. Then, too, there's almost a billion-dollar unclosed account on some lend-lease items sent Murmansk way during the Second World War. Well, anyway, there'll be a few Israeli oranges in Russian tea in the next few years, even if they do end up on the luncheon table for the Egyptian Ambassador.

AND LEAVE THE DRIVING TO US

In Israel, where only eighteen people in every thousand own a car, buses are a big thing. Hardly a month goes by without the mention of expansion of the bus service and facilities or a squabble between the various municipal authorities and the bus cooperatives. Bus drivers are the Israeli élite. In a country of outspoken and independent personalities, they are by far the most outspoken and independent of all, so much so, that they have become a part of the national folklore and image.

By Israeli standards, they are extremely well paid. In some cases they own the buses they are driving. These two facts, combined with the daily onslaught of multilingual multitudes of perhaps the world's most impatient travelers, have hardened the Israeli bus driver into the man of iron he must be to constantly face his archenemy, Israeli traffic.

Riding an Israeli bus is an exhilarating experience, which many tourists unfortunately miss. Where else in the world can you obtain all the personal thrill and excitement of participating in a Le Mans race held in the Rocky Mountains in a giant-size racing car. Not only can you experience the thrill, but you can share it with the forty odd, and I mean odd, other passengers on the bus, something which no ordinary racing driver can do. As you sit there pinned to the seat by the centrifugal force created by swirling around curves, you can bask in the comfort of the knowledge that your driver has at least 10 per cent of his thoughts on the road. Ninety per cent of the time he is talking to the local *chaticha*.

There are some ugly anti-Zionist rumors afloat that Israeli buses are dirty. This is just not so. They are either filthy or immaculate. They just don't have time to pass through the plain dirty stage. Busses are cleaned frequently at irregular intervals and at times you may be lucky enough to ride on a spic and span vehicle. Actually, the general untidiness of the buses is part of the campaign of the bus companies to prepare you in case, heaven forbid, you should have to use their so-called sanitary facilities.

During the tourist off-season, the Israeli public gets the chance to ride in some of the lovely special tourist buses. These are positive delights with reclining seats, headrests, air-conditioning, and all the comforts of Greyhound, sans dog. These buses are usually restricted to the more urbanized areas since their owners are likely to be a little more sensitive to goat dung and chicken feathers on the upholstery. In some areas, one gets the impression that the Bedouins have abandoned the ship of the desert for the Leyland Corporation and are doing their nomadic wandering on fourteen wheels.

Whether it be the driver, the passengers, or the bus, transportation in Israel is more than going from place to place. Unfortunately, it's usually an adventure.

SHADES OF TOM SAWYER

If nothing else rubs off on you, on your trip to Israel, you can be sure the walls will. In most countries, walls are built to shield; in Israel, they're built to shed.

Tom Sawyer could have a year-round job here, white-washing. Even the most luxurious homes in the country come with whitewashed walls, which gives them a hospital-like antiseptic look. Looking isn't bad; it's brushing or bumping into that becomes a problem.

Eighty per cent of our clothing usually has at least one white mark on it, where we scraped against the walls. Sometimes, of course, the whitewash rubs off in the most provocative places, which has considerably enhanced the sport of wench-watching.

Alas, progress is rearing its ugly head and Israelis are becoming increasingly "plastic" paint conscious. These "plastic" paints are water soluble and, along with their durability, they do not rub off. If, however, they are painted directly over the whitewash, they have a tendency to pop off in sheets, which gives your walls a nice patchwork effect.

You can cover this up, of course, with wallpaper. But then the entire wall will probably disintegrate in a few years from the entrapped humidity.

NO PROBLEMS

Not too long ago an excellent book on Israel was written by Roy Elston, an English newspaper correspondent who spent many years in the country. It derived its title, *No Alternative,* from the Hebrew *Ein Brerah,* which was the watchword during the years of struggle against the Arabs and the British Mandatory Government.

Ein Brerah is still heard occasionally in Israel, but frankly I believe it has been supplanted and surpassed by another more up-to-date and appropriate phrase, *lo baya* ("no problem"). Say you are building a house in Israel. The builder and the architect, being of different political views, don't really speak to each other and the house is completed without piping in the bathroom. Problem? *Lo baya.* Just rip the wall out and install the plumbing.

The number of things that are no problem in Israel are legion. From the average conversation it would seem that the entire Israeli economy is affluent and worry-free, the neighbors of Israel are all on the most cordial relations and doing their utmost to help the state, and no sociological conflicts are occurring to steam up the pressure cooker.

Maybe it's a welcome spirit of confidence and growth. A people have come a long way if they can say instead of no alternative, no problem — even if it isn't true.

KEROSENE KAPERS

Israel has often been described as a pressure cooker instead of a melting pot. The fuel that warms the cooker is bound to be kerosene. At the turn of the century, most oil was distilled to yield kerosene, and gasoline only took over in the early 1900's. Well, I don't know if gasoline has yet completely won the battle for supremacy in Israel. Kerosene manufacture, distribution, and consumption is still a big factor in the Israeli economy.

There was a time when everybody cooked on small primus or kerosene stoves. These have generally gone by the wayside now, but kerosene room, or "fireside," heaters are still an everyday household item in central-heatless Israel.

As a Midwesterner who spent some time in -38° Minnesota, you'd think Israeli winters, which only occasionally drop to 40° above, would be a pushover. Frankly, we've never been so cold in our lives. We go around bundled in layers of flannel shirts and sweaters, and we bury ourselves under comforters at night.

Our first and only line of defense against the cold are our two faithful, and one just so-so, kerosene heaters. They were sold to us last year by the Englishman who runs the corner hardware store. He just couldn't understand why we were totally unfamiliar with the whole principle of kerosene heating. It's quite a tortuous puzzle.

First you have to get the kerosene, or *neft*, as it is called in Hebrew (from which, incidentally, the English word "naptha" is derived). There are two ways to go about this. One is to shiver in silence until the *neft* man comes along ringing his bell like a gas-soaked town crier and pulling a 55-gallon barrel of *neft* with a one-horsepower, four-footed engine. Since the *neft* man hates cold weather and usually shows up on the brightest, hottest days, it's best not to wait around. The other way is to put your newly acquired jerry cans into your car and fill-em-up at the *neft* pump in the gas station. Some gas stations have a bad habit of playing hopscotch with their *neft* pumps, which adds that extra thrill to the heating business, as you never know when you may get gasoline instead.

Assuming you have finally found the correct fluid, there is the problem of putting it in your container. The kerosene-soaked flagstones on our terrace are mute evidence to my ineptitude as a jerry-can juggler. Once the majority, or at least some of the *neft,* is in the burner can, you turn it upside down and set it in your heater. It has a special valve that is guaranteed not to leak upside down, but just accidentally bump it and you get a gushing, gurgling fountain.

After you have safely deposited the *neft* can in your heater, you open the valve and allow the wick to sop up the kerosene. In case the wick does not do this, you consult the instructions, which are useless, since they are in Hebrew and German and thus unintelligible.

Finally the wick gets soaking and you apply a match. A thick sooty flame engulfs you and you grope for the chimney that slides over the wick. This device, which is essentially a piece of screen wire, acts as an afterburner and gives a clean (choke) smokeless flame.

After two weeks of headache and nausea, you finally remember to keep your window open at night; but in about two months, you get used to smelling like a grilled grease monkey and the odors of freshly picked oranges and freshly lit kerosene mingle lightly in your nostrils. By this time, however, it's getting so hot you wish you'd brought that air-conditioner along. Anyway, with the warm weather, the kerosene man is always here on time.

MUSIC TO CREEP BY

Detroit has one of the largest Arabic populations in America, with about 10,000 Lebanese and Syrians. There are three genuine mosques, not counting the Black Muslim ones. When we lived there one of our occasional pleasures was to visit some of the Arabic night clubs, which featured belly dancers (mostly from Brooklyn) for the eye and lovely exotic music for the ear. We even got to like the music so well that we'd listen to it Sunday afternoons on the Lebanese hour on the radio.

Here in Israel we have rapidly become disenchanted with Arabiana. With almost the entire radio spectrum jammed with Arabic broadcasts from Cairo to Damascus, we can get our Arab hour at any time and, frankly, now we feel, Who wants it? In America Arab music sounds mysterious and alluring; here in the Middle East it's just miserable and chaotic. Once in a while a melody will appeal to the Western ear, but the majority of the singers sound like they're being prompted with a jasmine tipped scimitar. A few hours of these desert ditties make you want to crawl up the walls.

There is nothing racist or nationalistic in my dislike of Arab music, nor is it a typical Israeli attitude. Most immigrants from the Arab countries and North Africa are fans and keep their transistors tuned to the neighboring stations. I suppose Israeli tunes are just as foreign and unpleasant to the Arab. I guess it depends on your current situation. There is, however, one musical common denominator between both worlds, which is heard in profusion on all stations — rock and roll.

KOLBOINIK

Every language has a few outstandingly descriptive words that seem to fuse sound, symbolism, and meaning into one sonorous whole. *Kolboinik* is such a word. It comes from three roots: *kol*, meaning "everything"; *bo*, meaning "comes" or "come to"; and *nick*, which is a Yiddish-Hebrew-Russian suffix. It means then "everything comes into it," and is the colloquial word for garbage can.

We had our own special *kolboinik*. It was a he. He was a stray, semi-wild dog, whom we acquired with the first home we rented in Israel. Israel is full of such dogs: they look like a cross between a German shepherd and a domesticated jackal. These lean, tawny creatures are found in and around the outskirts of the smaller cities and villages in central Israel, and rumor has it that they cross over the border between Jordan and Israel because Israel has recently begun producing a higher quality garbage.

On our first night in a strange home and a still strange land, we were glad to hear the reassuring bark of a dog in answer to the then terrifying jackal screams, and we did not regret feeding all our garbage scraps to our self-appointed canine companion. He did not, however, get his name Kolboinik until the next day. We had moved into our home a few days before Yom Kippur and I made arrangements to procure a seat in the local synagogue. The chairman of the synagogue called on us the day after we moved in, I paid for my seat, and then forgot about the whole matter until the next day when I couldn't locate my wallet. It did not take very long to conduct a complete search of our almost empty premises. My wallet was not to be found. That afternoon my little daughter brought in a masticated bit of leather that looked suspiciously like it might have been a wallet in days gone by.

A search of the general outside area confirmed our worst fears. There in shreds lay pieces of leather, social security cards, a draft card, and thank goodness, chewed but not shredded Israeli bank notes. We collected the debris and clearly ascertained the jaw and teeth marks of man's best friend. The only bill really badly torn was the lone fifty pound note, Israel's highest denomination of currency. We certainly had a high-priced pet on the premises. I can't remember if I returned the still edible wallet to the dog at that time, but I do know this was when he acquired his name.

Kolboinik was destined to play a big role in our lives during our first weeks in Israel. He had gotten off to an outstanding start, but we kept him anyway. Did you ever try to get rid of a sad-eyed starving mongrel?

After a few nights, the jackal howls no longer bothered us, and we became increasingly aware of the barking, yelping, and yowling that Kolboinik conducted as part of his nightly vigilance. It grew worse as Kolboinik's reputation as a new, well-fed Don Juan spread.

He soon learned how to get into the house himself, and when at times he wasn't successful, he left lovely deep paw marks on the door sills. We could put up with him; our friends could not. One fateful morning my wife and children called on an American neighbor about a mile away. Kolboinik, a sociable animal, followed them down the road and, to our neighbor's horror, into her house.

He immediately lit out for a comfortable place underneath one of the beds and all efforts to dislodge him were met with terrifying snorts and snarls. A few people love wild dogs, most avoid them, and some, like our neighbor, are terrified of them. With Kolboinik threatening her home and her children, she called up the local authorities, who sent over their local *shomer,* or watchman, to remove the beast.

This pistol packing ex-partisan had a little watchdog of his own the size of a Shetland pony, and perhaps because he wanted to eliminate the competition, he decided it would be wisest for all concerned to shoot poor Kolboinik. So in full view of the children, he drew his pistol, clutched Kolboinik by the neck, and marched him off to the orange orchard. Two shots were heard;

the valiant *shomer* strode from the orchard blowing on his smoking gun; and so that was Kolboinik's end — or almost.

That afternoon, when I came home to an uncommonly quiet household, I asked my wife what had happened to Kolboinik. She gave me the let's-not-talk-about-it-when-the-children-are-around look, so I dropped the matter and went out to relax on the patio. There on the lawn, not ten feet away, lay a dog. He was perfectly still, his four legs rigidly pointing to the sky. He looked like Kolboinik, but then most dogs around here did. I went over to verify the body. I nudged him gently with my foot. There was no response.

When I told my wife of the carcass on our lawn, she was terrified: Kolboinik had been shot that morning at our friend's house, a good mile down the road. He had obviously been wounded and had come back here, his home, to die. Cursing the *shomer*, I returned to the yard with a shovel to bury poor Kolboinik.

Kolboinik wasn't about to be buried. The stiff legs suddenly relaxed; one canine iris opened wide and gazed at me and the shovel. With a bounding leap, our dead friend was all over the property. Howling us to sleep that night, we felt that this superb animal-actor had earned a reprieve, and Kolboinik became a member of the family again.

The next morning we were awakened by two shots. By the side of the road stood the *shomer*, Wyatt Earp of the Middle East, his gun smoking. His target, Kolboinik, who was not more than thirty feet away, was dashing helter-skelter for the back of the house, a flesh wound through the nape of the neck. Kolboinik survived this attack, but his faith in mankind faltered and he began to snarl at little children. Eventually he went the way of all dogs, and some months later we moved from the house to our permanent home.

The new tenants of our old home have a dog they call Felafel. In his new abode, he has acquired a new companion, a lean, tawny semi-wild creature, who seems to belong to the house. They haven't named him yet.

GIVE AND TELL

There was a time when you had to be a hero, a tyrant, or at least a politician, to have a city named after you. In modern Israel it's much easier: all you have to do is buy it — well, maybe "found it" is the right expression, although a founder of a city usually lives in it for some time. Here in Israel, if you buy and develop enough land to create a fair-sized community and are an American philanthropist of note, you can have the place named after you for a little extra donation.

Naming a city after the donor is probably the epitome of the give-and-tell syndrome that has developed in Anglo-American-Israeli philanthropy. I think it all began way back when, with the trees.

Every boy who went to Hebrew school in America remembers the manila cards with the trees printed on them. There was space for twenty-five leaves on this pine-palm synthesis, and each time you contributed a dime to the Jewish National Fund, your teacher gave you a green leaf stamp to stick on the tree. Twenty-five stamps and you had a sapling ready for planting in the holy soil with your name on it . . . or so we thought.

During the tourist season in Israel hundreds of nice Hadassah ladies are horrified to learn that the trees they planted as children or in later years as gifts for weddings, bar mitzvahs, etc., do not bear plaques inscribed with their names. But when you stop to rationalize, it becomes obvious that you just can't tend both a plaque and a tree for twenty years for two dollars.

Trees, however, are the rare exception. Anything else that is donated to Israel has, upon request, a name that goes with it. In some charitable institutions every desk, table, chair, stool, room, and bedpan has a plaque with the donor's name engraved on it. This may be excellent for the plaque industry, but it drives the poor institution personnel to distraction when a busload of tourists descend upon it. A horde of American plaque-mad philanthropists descending upon a religious institution to which they had donated was one of the least memorable events of my visit here as a tourist. Luckily, none of the classes were in session, for I am sure the students would have been removed bodily from their chairs by the transfixed donors seeking the evidence of their share in the Holy Land.

According to Maimonides, in the highest form of charity the donor does not know the recipient and the recipient does not know the donor. Well, anyway, let's be thankful some name-dropping multibillionaire did not contribute a couple of billion to the state, or we might be living in Katzland.

V

Bar Mitzvak
Country Style

HUP, TWO, THREE, FOUR

The recruiting office is so well hidden that the Jordanians will never find it. Unfortunately, neither do most Israelis. I understand that part of the bar mitzvah training of an Israeli boy is teaching him how to locate the place.

About a week after I received that postcard, I finally found the office, hidden away in the jungles of Petach Tikva.

"Look," I said to the policeman at the entrance, "I'm an American citizen and I . . . "

"Sit down on the bench next to the door marked eight."

"But I . . . "

"Door eight."

I read William Saroyan's autobiography, five recruiting posters, and memorized the Jerusalem *Post*. Finally my name was called.

"Name? Birthplace? Identity Card? Sign here."

"But I'm an American citizen and American law forbids serving in a foreign army."

"Sign here."

"I . . . I . . . "

"You won't sign?"

"I'd like to consult with the American Embassy."

"Never mind, we'll sign for you. You're in Israel and not in America. Come back tomorrow at 8:00 A.M. for your physical."

"But I'm an American . . ."

"Eight A.M."

The next morning I was hopeful. Surely one of the Middle Eastern maladies I had contracted would free me of this madness.

"Cough."

I coughed.

"Again."

Do you cough different in Hebrew? Maybe from right to left? I coughed.

"Again."

I coughed. A woman doctor yet.

"Have you ever had bilharzia, glaucoma, or sickle cell anemia?"

"But I'm an American citizen and . . ."

"Please answer the question."

"No."

"You're in perfect health, *kin ein hora*" ("without the evil eye"), the doctor said as she spit twice over her left shoulder to ward off any demons. "Go to psychological testing in Room 206."

"Name?"

"Did you ever serve in the armed services of any other country before?"

"Look, I'm an American citizen and under American . . ."

"Were you in the American Army?"

"I was in the United States Marine Corps," I announced, sucking in my belly.

"Rank."

"Private First Class, which is equivalent, I believe, to a Lieutenant Colonel in the Israeli Army."

"Here, read this."

It was a beautiful piece of Hebrew poetry (I think) but since it wasn't written by King David, I could only make out two words.

"What's it about?" the interviewer asked.

"About rain, I think."

"You're a functional Hebrew moron, but report to Room 209B on Thursday, 7:30 A.M. We can still use you."

"But I'm an American citizen and . . ."

"Room 209B, Thursday, 7:30 A.M."

The fateful day dawned. I arrived at 7:32, well equipped this time with *Gone With the Wind* and the *Viking Portable Encyclopedia*. I had burned Atlanta and gotten down to Xerography when my name was called.

The little man at the desk didn't give me a chance to speak.

"I've got your files here, Mr. Geduld. You're in excellent health, you're Hebrew is a little weak but . . ."

"But I'm . . ."

"Please Mr. Geduld; but, unfortunately, you're an American citizen and you're not allowed to serve in the Israeli Army. Please come back here next year to check your status. *Shalom.*"

"*Shalom,*" I gasped, clutching my passport.

HAIRY TALES

Along with stamp stores, book stores, and sidewalk coffee houses, Israel has a profusion of barbershops. Maybe it's the frantic expansion rate of the country or maybe it's just the hot sun, but in Israel your hair grows like mad. The average man who takes a haircut every two weeks in the States will need one every week here if he wishes to maintain the equivalent grooming standard.

But despite the number of miracles that have occurred in this portion of the planet in past and present, if you come to Israel with a bare and polished dome, you will not, alas, grow new hair.

Hair styles for men run from the sublime to the ridiculous. The average Israel hair style for men can be described in one word, shaggy — the majority of the population finds weekly haircuts too expensive.

My wife first noticed the profusion of hair that grows out of men's ears. In America my barbers used to make discreet snips in the middle of a haircut, but in Israel the ear seems to be sacrosanct.

Some of the barbershops in Tel Aviv are the epitome of modernity, with the best in American and European tonsorial gadgetry to satisfy the most exotic tastes. Others, such as the one in Lod located near the regional abbatoir, are butchershops where the handclipper and aseptic pencil are still king.

Like their compatriots the world over, barbers in Israel are here to inform as well as to perform, and a session in a three-chair shop in Tel Aviv may result in a multilingual babble and wrangle on anything from the latest local scandal to an American election.

There is one thing still missing in Israeli barbershops: a number of establishments I used to frequent in Cleveland were also flourishing bookie joints with more scratch sheets than shaves, and the thrill of the illicit was added to the experience of getting a haircut. Israel has not yet progressed to the ponies, but, who knows, there's an awful lot of flat land in the Negev.

AN ENGLISH LEGACY

Of the many legacies the British government left in Israel, such as King George avenues, police stations, and Barclay's banks, none is as conspicuous as the abandoned army bases. A casual survey gives the impression that Palestine of the time was an armed camp, which, of course, it was — and is.

The British, or perhaps their Jewish contractors, were good builders. When they put something up, they expected it to last and last, which it did — mostly. Just south of Haifa is an army camp which immediately after the War of Liberation served as a reception center for new immigrants. After twelve or thirteen years of almost continuous use, it was finally abandoned and now the concrete is slowly being scavenged away. As the city develops, it will probably be totally razed for new housing projects.

Most bases have fared better. Some, like Sarafend, still function as army bases and twenty years have not greatly diminished the usefulness of the brick and concrete quonset-like huts that are the principal architectural features. Others have been turned into hospitals, social welfare agencies, and similar institutions.

What are really appealing — or appalling, depending upon your esthetic tastes — are the abandoned bases in the remote countryside. One such place is a former Marbara just a few kilometers south of Zichron Yaakov. Row after row of doorless, windowless, and in many instances roofless, barracks slash violently against the blue Israeli sky. What were once streets teeming with troops and later with immigrants are overgrown avenues of brick and rubble. All the English signs have long since been obliterated, but stark block Hebrew letters indicate former dining halls, living barracks, and offices.

Suddenly this isolated oasis comes alive. In the corner of one not-quite empty building an aged crinkled crone sweeps out a destroyed doorway with an old broom. In a camp that housed thousands she and her husband are the last survivors. How did she get here? Why does she remain here? Who knows. Perhaps like many of the temporary residents of this place so much of her life had been spent in camps that no other home seemed real to her.

Someone once wrote that Jews are the chameleons of mankind. And how. Israel is mankind in miniature.

Take the Herr Doktor Professor Engineer Krause. While I was in his office, his sidekick kept bowing and clicking his heels—Ja, Herr Doktor; Ja, Herr Doktor—just like the old German movies.

Or the Burmese fellow that works down in the warehouse. You didn't know there were Burmese Jews? Neither did I. He's about the most Burmese-looking Burmese I can imagine, and there, hanging on the wall, a picture of Queen Elizabeth mounted sidesaddle on her charger, taking the salute on Empire Day. This boy has brought the British Raj right with him.

His neighbors, the Indian Jews, are among the most colorful of the ingathered with their sweeping saris and their quiet dignity.

The Greek dockworkers and fishermen with their dances and restaurants, the English with their bowling greens, the Kurds with their fantastic flowing robes, the Persians who arrive with one wife and four carpets (or is it the other way around?), the Turks with the huge mustaches—Israel is a land where everyone has brought it with him.

Who's that nut on my front lawn trying to hit a white leather-covered ball with a stick?

What will emerge from this infusion of cultures? Well, unfortunately, khaki doesn't retain much individuality.

THIS PEOPLE ISRAEL

The gathering of worldwide Jewry into Israel has been accomplished with smoothness and lack of friction. People of totally different environmental, economic, and social backgrounds have been integrated into one community. There are, however, many exceptions, most of them private or local, that do not attract worldwide attention; but one which did is the situation of the Jews from India, the Bene Israel.

Indian Jewry consists of two separate communities: the Bagdad Jews, who immigrated there in the early part of the nineteenth century; and a much older group, of about 10,000 people, the Bene Israel, who left Judea before the Maccabean revolt in 175 B.C.E. in order to escape the persecutions of Antiochus Epiphanes, the Syrio-Greek ruler. Their ship floundered in a storm off the Konchin coast, about thirty miles south of the present-day city of Bombay. The survivors of the shipwreck found themselves without their most precious possession, their Sefer Tora, which was lost at sea.

Because of this major misfortune, they developed in ignorance of the Hebrew language, and through the millennia of their miraculous survival, they retained only the *Shema* ("Here, O Israel the Lord our God, the Lord is One"), which they recited on all religious occasions. Between five and nine hundred years after their arrival in India, a half-legendary character by the name of David Rahabi found the remnants of this community and taught them, or retaught them, the essences of Judaism.

With the establishment of the State of Israel, a number of these Bene Israel emigrated to Israel, where they were at first accepted with open arms. Soon, however, because of their somewhat loose tradition of Orthodox Judaism, certain religious authorities in Israel, including the higher rabbinate, forbade marriage between the Bene Israel and other Jews unless they could give certain proofs of their Jewish ancestry.

Although this attitude smacks of racism to most of the liberal Israeli population, there is a strong element who justify its adoption. Perhaps most vociferous among them have been the Bagdad Jews, who have brought to Israel some of the caste-ridden prejudice so prevalent in India.

All this was of little consequence to me until I became friendly with a young Indian boy. He was a proud scion of one of Indian Jewry's best-known families and prided himself on his Bagdadi background. As it must come to all men, he finally decided to marry. His bride-to-be was an Iraqi girl of wealthy parentage. Before his father-in-law would let him join the roost, he made the boy prove his parentage. He wasn't going to let his daughter marry into any semi-Jewish family.

It is seldom realized how often public policies are private miseries. If the rabbinate realized how much grief and heartache their policy on the Bene Israel problem brought to innocent people, I'm sure they'd have a complete and immediate change of heart.

In order to prove his Jewishness, my friend had to bring two witnesses to the local chief rabbinate office. Under slight duress, I volunteered, and after donning the appropriate handkerchief headpiece, was led into the rabbi's presence. The rabbi turned out to be a thoughtful, patient man who didn't like his task any more than my friend who was questioned. My testimony was worthless since I had known Eli only in Israel and what they wanted were witnesses who had known him from boyhood in India.

After much rigamarole, it finally turned out that my friend's uncle had long been a respected member of the local religious community. Eli's Jewishness was decided to be beyond reproach.

They are happily married now and the incident is just a part of the, let's hope, soon-to-be-forgotten past.

TRAMPISTIM

Years ago when I served my hitch in the U.S. Glory Corps, I used to negotiate my way from Great Lakes to Cleveland and back by the time-honored technique of the thumb. This mode of travel was once of paramount importance in Israel, but as the country prospers, it is slowly succumbing to public and private transportation. Still, every day, and especially every Friday afternoon, the roads and intersections are filled with young people in search of a lift. True, there are many grizzled oldtimers who would rather hitch than pay, but the overall impression the passing motorist gets is one of youth on the move.

If age plays a part, sex plays none at all. Young girls in and out of uniform, and in every type of costume from tight stretch pants to dainty country dresses, look for rides without any apparent embarrassment or fear. Can you imagine a single girl of twenty-one traveling alone at night on a country road in America and hitching a ride with a stranger?

The Hebrew colloquial for hitchhiker is derived from the English expression "to tramp a ride": hitchhikers are called *trampistim*. There was a time when everybody picked up anybody, but this spirit is rapidly disappearing and sometimes you may wait up to a half hour for a lift. Most chronic hitchhikers in Israel are a hardy lot, and if you're going anywhere in the general direction, they'll hitch along hoping to find another lift somewhere to their specific destination. I have had *trampistim* ride with me for miles out of their way just because they feel half a lift is better than none.

No trampist will ever stick out his thumb in stateside fashion. Gensus Trampistus Israelianus is divided into four main phylla: the looker, the gesticulator, the frenzied waver, and the sign painter. The looker is the cream of the hitchhike world. She (it usually is a she) just gazes somewhat disdainfully at passing traffic with a you-know-I'm-here-why-the-hell-don't-you-stop look. And stop they do, in droves, for this Middle East Evil Eye Fleagle. If you should commit the cardinal sin of passing them, these gals have a gaze cold enough to chill your brake fluid.

The gesticulator uses a typical Arabic gesture that is anathema to my still somewhat Western mind. The thumb is brought forward to meet the middle finger and the other fingers are wrapped around it. Then the whole hand is moved up and down from the elbow, giving the impression of a gyrating goose's neck. For me, the gesture sums up all that is slimy and slovenly about the Levantine mind. Be that as it may, the gesticulator is picked up readily.

The frenzied waver is usually the G.I. on a weekend pass. Since the Israeli weekend consists of Friday afternoon and Saturday, this boy is in a hurry. He's going to stop the next car or drop dead trying. Unfortunately, the latter occurs quite often. These boys stand out in the middle of the road waving their arms, head, and legs in a frantic effort to stop the next passing auto. When you first spot them in action, you get the idea that they are either learning the Charleston or trying to kill themselves. You are so busy trying to avoid them and cursing their obstructive presence that you seldom stop to pick them up.

The sign painter is the only practical man in the lot. He merely indicates his destination on a small rectangular white card which he holds up in front of himself. For the benefit of the many tourists, these are usually bilingual, English and Hebrew. An ambitious trampist could guarantee himself fast, direct transportation by writing a multilingual destination card with Hebrew, English, French, Spanish, Italian, Arabic, and perhaps Japanese, characters.

LIFTS

If I gave it any passing thought at all, I associated the noun
"lift" with the British term for elevator. Actually, lift has forty-
three different meanings. None of them describe the object
referred to in Israel.

A lift is the huge box in which the new immigrant brings
all his worldly goods to Israel (if he's lucky).

Lifts come in all sizes, shapes, and materials. The average
size is about 6 by 4 by 10 feet, but some are so gigantic that
they block the Jerusalem road when they're being brought up.
The majority of lifts are made of a cheap grade of wood, but
I have seen some exotic ones. One friend of mine had his built
of mahogany boards, which he used for shelving in his new
home and thus got it in the country duty free—a fantastic
achievement. Some embassy personnel lifts are huge, reusable
steel cases, and, come to think of it, make excellent shelters.

Our lifts (which I, of course, didn't know were lifts) were of
a cheap grade of wood. Two of them disintegrated at the Haifa
port when they were inadvertently lowered from the ship without
the aid of a winch. (I should complain? My neighbor's lifts
you ever squeezed salt water out of five-hundred books?) Anyway, the port authorities were real princes about the matter.
They had the top and bottom of my lifts, with as much of the
innards as they could assemble, locked in a screened-off area of
the warehouse.

We had about eight lifts intact. After the destructive scenes
at customs, they were loaded, under bribe, on a huge flat-bed
truck. I sat next to the driver and we made it home from Haifa
through sixteen different gears and a pouring rain. I was so
glad to get our stuff that I just dumped the empty crates back
on the truck and let the driver haul them away. You get too
soon old and too late smart. Each lift was worth about I£ 70,

a fortune in Israel. In the town next to us, one serves as a small general store. They are factories, workshops, stalls, homes, and barns. They also make marvelous doll houses, and let's hope the Israeli economy reaches the stage when that's all they'll be used for.

I see by the new Random House Dictionary of the English Language that five high class Yiddishisms have made the big time—schlepp, schlock, schmaltz, schmoose, and yep, schmuck—and all on page 1277. I was actually looking for the word *schmatte*, which unfortunately has not made it, so I'll explain it here. You want the other meanings? Go look them up. A dictionary I am not writing.

Anyway, a *schmatte* is a glorified rag. How glorified I was not to realize until we moved to Israel. The Yiddish *schmatte,* I have now etymologically ascertained, must have come from the Hebrew word *smartut,* which sounds Israeli but still means a rag. But what a rag. A *smartut* is a heavy yard-square rag, woven of thick absorbent fibre, which serves as swab, sponge, and mop.

The lovely American string mop, which is often substituted for a hairdo on Halloween, or the prosaic sponge mop are unknown in Israel. The *smartut* is scientifically wrapped around the end of a T-shaped stick and, surprisingly, it does a superb job of swabbing up the stone floors. It also has made a painless transition into the twentieth century and is outstanding for washing your car.

There must be some deep psychological reason for the continued and overwhelming popularity of the *smartut*. Perhaps it lies in the emotional release the cleaning lady gets as she wrathfully wrings the last bit of water out of the thick necklike folds of the coiled *smartut* or the resounding sound a wet *smartut* makes when it is slapped on a wet floor. Anyway, my wife soon abandoned the sponge mops we had foolishly brought over in our lifts and settled under the *smartut* spell.

There is one drawback to the *smartut*: it kind of slops over on the furniture legs and after a few months all your furniture will be the bleached victims of alkali attack.

A merchandizing madman could find a fertile field in the *smartut* market. Currently, they are all a dismal grey color. I can envision more modern *smartutim*, in lovely pastel shades. The gals here would wring it up.

THE PLAY WAS A WASHOUT

One of the many marvelous things brought about by the creation of the State of Israel has been the revival of old festival customs which were only marginally observed in the Diaspora. One such custom is the *Purim Shpiel,* or Purim Play, which adds to the festivities of that most festive of Hebrew holidays, Purim.

Last year the local ladies put on an outstanding adaptation of *My Fair Lady* (Queen Esther, naturally). This year, the Purim lot fell on me and we put on a play I had written called *Benedict,* which delves into the degradations meted out by American tourists to the local folk, and vice versa. We will spare you a further description of the play; this little saga is about opening night in Israel, as seen through the eyes of the writer, producer-director, stagehand, carpenter, and buttcan boy.

The rehearsals went well enough. We even managed on occasion to gather together all fourteen people who were scheduled to be in the play. The dress rehearsal went flawlessly, with one exception: the main character, who has only one line at the end of the play, botched it, but he promised to do better on opening night. Finally after intensive preparations, the big night came.

The performance was held in our synagogue hall. (Luckily the rabbi had not been present at any of the rehearsals or, as he said later, he probably would have radically censored it.) The stage was lit by two rented spotlights which had worked perfectly the previous night. Twenty minutes before show time we turned on the spots. Bamm! A light popped. We had one spare. We screwed it in. Bamm! We were spotless.

The show was due to go on in fifteen minutes, and as I was painfully plucking the remaining tufts of my bald pate one of the sisterhood ladies came by with a huge coffee urn. "What's that for?" I groaned.

"Tea for the cast."

"Tea! Who needs tea! We need lights! Be careful how you plug that in."

She was, and blew every fuse in the house. We now had a pitch black theater rapidly filling with people, one unworkable spotlight, and a palpitating producer. Aware of the idiocyncrasies of Israeli electrical systems, I had at the last minute brought my newly acquired, French bottled-gas camping lantern with me to the theater, and by the light of flickering cigarette lighters managed to get it lit and locate the fuse box.

The main fuse was gone, and after a few minutes of multilingual madness I managed to make my plight known to the Electric Company's service department in Petach Tikva. They promised to send a man out right away. Meanwhile, someone had called Fifi Fixit, our local handyman, and he appeared on the scene just as I hung up after talking to the electricity people.

"What?" he said. "You called the Electric Company? Now I can't fix the fuse. I can't break the seal of their box."

After much pleading and persuasion, Fifi reevaluated his fuse-box morality, broke the seal, replaced the fuse, and we had lights. Incidentally, we never did have tea.

The spotlight dilemma was solved by the procurement of an old outside terrace light from the leading lady's back porch, and though twenty minutes late we were all set to go—we thought.

The curtain pullers—we had tried an automated rig, which promptly collapsed—were a helpful husband-and-wife team, Moishe and Adrianne, who lived close to the synagogue. We were about to pull the curtains when a breathless British accent plunged backstage, gasped, and said: "I've got to see Moishe."

"But you can't, he's pulling the curtain just now."

"But he's being flooded!"

"Flooded?"

"One of the cars trying to park for the play broke the water main in front of his house and the water is spouting out like a geyser."

We pulled the curtains anyway. Moishe's lawn floated away during the first act.

MUSTAPHA

Israel has a compulsory education law that requires all kids up to the age of fourteen to attend school. But in the Arab community, this law is breached more than it is observed. Every morning I drive behind truckloads of colorfully dressed Arab children being hauled to farms and plantations in the area to pick fruit or plant produce. Perhaps Arab kids look very young at fourteen, but very few of the children in the trucks look old enough to be Bar Mitzvah.

There is one underage hooky player in Israel whom I have come to know quite well, for two people who can't communicate. He is a little Bedouin boy of nine, who with his sister of seven, is in charge of shepherding his family's flock of eighty-odd sheep in the Lydda area. Certainly the self-reliance he has learned in the fields could not be taught him in any school. Where is the American family who would entrust their entire fortune, in this case $2,000 to $3,000, to a nine-year-old boy?

His name is Mustapha and he speaks Hebrew only under protest, so we communicate with each other mainly by grunts, groans, and fingers. He has achieved some status of manhood because he wears shoes; his sister still runs around barefoot in the 38° cold.

He doesn't own a shepherd's staff or a shepherd's flute, but controls his brood with an untraditional but effective four-foot coiled strip of one-quarter inch steel. Whenever one of his flock goes astray, he sends this steel hoop sailing into its back end, which soon puts the wayward sheep on the right track. His sister really doesn't have her heart in the work yet. She spends most of her time rolling her hoop in and out among the olive trees and only occasionally is concerned with the flock's welfare.

Mustapha's biggest occupation is staring. He spends most of his days just looking at an alien world growing up around him. I meet him when I go out into the field behind our factory to eat lunch. First his sheep appear over the crest of the ridge and then slowly, circuitously move toward me. They seem to be headed for a choice pasturage under an olive tree twenty feet away when they suddenly veer and surround me. I don't particularly relish a sheep's company at lunch (except in the form of lamb chops), especially since these woolly tailed vagabonds are prepared to devour my sandwiches, my oranges, my waxpaper, and perhaps even my lunchbox.

A few loud *kishes* (Arab for "take off") usually clears the baaing mass from my lunch area, but recently one managed to knock over my glass of tea. Some of the more demonstrative sheep demonstrate their disgust at my inhospitality by gushing loudly and voluminously on the spot. Once my appetite is thus thoroughly crushed, I spend the rest of my lunch break exchanging stares with Mustapha, who has now appeared to dispel his impolite charges.

The grazing area for Mustapha's sheep is becoming increasingly constrained by *shikunim*, factories, orange groves, and roads, but somehow he will survive. One can't imagine the country of David without its shepherds.

CANDLELIGHT DINNERS

One of the things we like most, or perhaps more correctly, least, about living in Israel are the candlelight dinners we have to attend. Not that we mingle in high social circles or with the diplomatic corps; we just happen to live in an area where the lights are continually blacking out.

Israel intends to invest a tremendous fortune in manpower and materials to produce atomic power cheaply in the Negev. Someday I hope she will short circuit a little of this investment to keep her conventional electric power burning on a better schedule.

The main producers of soft-light living are the electrical storms in winter. Just let a stray bolt of lightning strike anywhere within the bounds of the ancient kingdom of Judah and boom, the transformer down the block draws the bolt magnetically to her, giving up our power in a lover's kiss.

It wouldn't be so frustrating if everybody's power went off. I don't even mind them having a little extra light at Lydda airport, which is in viewing distance of our home, but what used to rail my nationalistic ire was to gaze upon the "underdeveloped seventeenth century" Arab villages in the ex-Jordanian hills and watch the lights twinkle on and off.

A couple of months ago we bought a newly marketed, locally produced electric clock to keep accurate time in our home. Sadly, the power usually goes out for a short stretch in the middle of the night with no one the wiser and another day of late arrivals dawns.

Unfortunately, we did not bring along a kerosene lamp with all our pioneering gear, but luckily we're well stocked on Shabbat candles. The other week, after a continual scourge of on-again-off-again power days our lights and power went off just three hours before Shabbat. We saw our neighbors' lights across the street, but thought nothing of it since power failures are very exclusive in Israel. However, when we found out that our neighbors on both sides of us had lights we began to wonder; after all, how exclusive can you get? We finally found out that we had blown the main fuse to our home, providing us for the first time with a do-it-yourself candlelight dinner.

CAMELS

———◄●►———

People just don't take to camels the way they do to horses. Camel breeding for the newly rich? Never! Camel racing? Maybe among the Berbers in the Sahara. Perhaps it's because the camel is such a homely, disdainful, aloof beast. Take to them or not, there are quite a few around in Israel.

There are occasional reports of wild camels in the Negev Desert, but most camels in Israel are in the company of Bedouins. The drier it gets, the more you're apt to come across these characters, because the government extends their grazing lands down to but not including (unless the guards aren't looking) the Tel Aviv public parks. Usually the camels are part of a happy Bedouin family consisting of a multitude of sheep, goats, chickens, kids, and dirt. Occasionally you'll see a whole caravan looking like a Christmas card come to life.

Aside from a tourist in Beersheba I don't think I've ever seen anyone actually riding a camel. Perhaps camel saddles are expensive or perhaps they're all sold for export, but the only thing I've seen on camels are bags and boxes.

There are no camel thieves here as there were hoss thieves in the Wild West, but there are camel traders. Every Thursday morning in Beersheba is camel swapping and market day for the Bedouins. Their ranks are thinning out, however, and a few decades may see the used camel dealer traded for the used Jeep dealer. It'll take some time though because mileage on a camel doesn't pile up too fast and maintenance costs are minimal.

One of the loveliest sights is a pure albino camel. These pink-eyed beasts are a photographer's dream silhouetted against an azure-blue sky or golden-brown sand dune. Camels should be cultivated by the Government Tourist Agency, for it would be sad indeed if the only camel the Israeli tourist saw was on his cigarette pack.

FILL 'ER UP YOURSELF

In America a place where gasoline is sold is generally known as a service station. That name is not applicable in Israel. If anything, what goes on in most Israeli gas stations is self-service. I think every Israeli, as part of his driving test, must take a course in the use and operation of a gasoline pump.

The Israeli motorist zooms into the benzine station (gasoline is a foreign term here), blows his horn, slams on his brakes, pulls his wife out of the windshield, and leaps out of the car to the closest benzine pump. He proceeds to fill his tank at a furious rate, screams at the proprietor, who shows up just in time to take his money, and zooms out in a flat four minutes. Wash your windshield? Clean your headlights? Unheard of. Sometimes, under protest, a station owner will check the oil for you and at times even the water but never, never, without your asking him first.

There are some heralds of change in this situation. The movement for gas station reform has sprung up, not from the occasional American who has settled here, but from Israelis who have spent time in the States and who are appalled at the contrast between Israeli and American stations. It's a tough fight though. One Israeli friend of mine, who trained a benzine station attendant to wipe his windshield, gave it up after awhile because he got tired of wiping off the oil slick.

My secret ambition has been to open up a sparkling benzine station with properly, or improperly, clad female gas jockeys who could fill tanks, check oil, water, batteries, and utterly rock the foundation of the Israeli benzine station business.

COUNTDOWN

In a country of immigrants how can you find out discreetly where a person comes from without asking him?

Listen to his accent? Maybe, if your ear is attuned to detect localities.

Let me tell you how I found out. One day the local press came out with screaming headlines (well, maybe they weren't screaming; in fact, I don't think they were even headlines, but I do know there was an article on it because it made a lasting impression on me): "The Secret Is Out, Ben Gurion Counts in Yiddish!"

In a fleeting moment of oversight the Security Services had permitted the incredible word to leak out. As Ben Gurion was being chauffeured from Jerusalem to Tel Aviv, one of his drivers overheard him counting something — trees, or goats, or bond sales, I forget what, but that is irrelevant — in Yiddish.

This then is how you know. A man may have come to Israel in the second aliyah, become its supreme leader, and a distinguished Hebrew linguist and writer, but when he counts, it's how he learned in *cheder*: *einz, tzvai, drii* . . .

With this piece of glorious information I set about making my own secret survey of national origins. First my boss: when he added up the results of a dust particle count (don't ask me to elaborate; a scientific treatise this is not) it was in his native Serbian. The girl at the checkout counter in the supermarket added up the bill in her native Romanian. In the restaurant where our family makes its once a month to-remember-how-it-was-when-we-ate-out-in-America pilgrimage, the proprietor calculated the tab in Persian. The gas station attendant made change in Arabic, and so on ad infinitum.

It's a good system. Only one drawback. To be adept at it in Israel, you had better learn how to count in at least forty or fifty different languages.

SQUEEZE PLAYS

———◄◦►———

Try to park a car in Tel Aviv and the following things are bound to occur. First, the loafer or sunseeker in the nearest doorway will get up off his perch and very professionally begin to guide you into your parking place. His hand- and sometimes his beard-waving signals are enough to crash land a full flight of planes on an Essex Class carrier, but all he manages to do is confuse you and draw everybody else's attention to your plight.

He is quickly joined by a fender watcher fourth-class, typically an eight- to ten-year-old kid whose main concern in life is your deliverance from traffic with the minimum fuss. He generally charts a collision course that is in direct conflict with your first director. After you finally park the damn thing, he will sit on it, scratch his initials in the paint with his saw-toothed slingshot, and play stick ball on the fender.

Once, after being painstakingly directed by a pair of the above characters for about ten minutes into a miniscule parking spot, I finally gave up in disgust and pulled out of the area. Their looks of rejection and bewilderment were terrifying to observe. I'm sure the old guy went home and beat his wife after this experience and the kid probably kicked the nearest cat.

The most impressive parking assistant, however, is the traffic stopper. He is obviously a disgruntled reservist who never quite fulfilled his ambition to become an M.P. As soon as he spots you trying to back into a spot, out he prances into full traffic, his hand held out ramrod straight, defying all oncoming cars from interfering with your maneuvers. His aplomb is unshaken by the honks, hoots, and toots of oncoming traffic and he remains adamant until you are safely secured.

Strange, in a country where the man in the street is usually in too much of a hurry to give you more than the time of day.

A TRASHY TALE

A short item in a recent newspaper may mark the beginning of the end of a unique Israeli tradition — the "share the garbage pail" plan. It seems that Israeli ingenuity has recently brought out a garbage disposal unit which, with the proper *protectzia*, should find its way into many of the new housing schemes being built in the country.

It will be sad if it does. One of the sweet joys of Israeli life is to tiptoe out to your garbage pail on a moonless night, silently open the cover, find it brimful as usual, and then, with finesse and dignity, drop your garbage in your neighbors' pail. Although we cannot ascertain this for certain, we have the definite feeling that this is a reciprocal plan, because many times we vaguely identify substances and smells in our garbage can which even in their decayed state seem foreign to our senses.

Not only are garbage pails in Israel shared by humans, but also by animals: cats, dogs, and depending upon the location, jackals. This inter-specie socialism is definitely frowned upon even in Israel, and ingenious devices have been fashioned to prevent it. A garbage can in Israel is not an old-fashioned American galvanized bucket or a new-fashioned plastic one. In the cities there are painted steel buckets, but out in the country-side they are veritable pillboxes.

When you buy a garbage can here you don't take it home in your car trunk. It would probably lift the front wheels off the ground. This refuse repository consists of a heavy steel can entombed in a thick steel and concrete outer shell with a steel top lid and a steel front door, from which the occasional collector removes the inner contents. It is delivered to your door by a rather tired ass and two equally lethargic drivers. After some hours of frantic negotiation, they finally deposit it in a semi-level condition next to your neighbors' receptacle, allowing you a prime opportunity to play the local garbage game.

Despite the formidable fortifications against feline penetration, an occasional clever cat will manage to paw open an improperly locked can and wallow in delight in its innards. These Houdinis of the cat world have perfected a technique that is almost human in unlatching cans, but, alas, their endeavors are only transient, as the stray dogs in the neighborhood soon take over.

Somewhere in the eaves of our home where we store all the excess junk we brought from America, we have a garbage disposal unit waiting to be installed. I don't know if we'll ever get around to doing it. We might miss a part of the fun that way.

I'LL HAVE MINE UPSIDE DOWN

At one time every American visitor to Israel faithfully brought with him at least three one-pound jars of instant coffee for his relatives. (In fact, it's still not such a bad idea, because the price of a pound of coffee in Israel is half a day's wages for the average guy.) But today Israeli coffee is every bit as good as American. The main concern of the Israeli about his coffee is in the drinking. Here is where he excells.

The ability to prepare an outstanding cup of coffee is looked upon with awe and it is an honor to have a secretary who can do so. I worked at one firm that had one of the most indolent lab assistants you can imagine, but could she make a cup of coffee! She was assured of life tenure in her job.

The real Israeli coffee lover will not lower his dignity to drink ordinary instant coffee. Instead he will concoct a version of the Middle Eastern medicant known as Turkish Coffee. This is a thick oleum-like liquid which is poured steaming hot into your glass and then proceeds to congeal before your eyes. In about twenty seconds half the glass settles into a residue of grounds. You drink it gingerly, filtering off any lighter weight elements between your teeth. This is powerful stuff and can alienate the alimentary canal of the uninitiated.

The real connoisseur spices his coffee with an alleged Arabian aphrodisiac called "hel." It would be nice to say it tastes like it, but it doesn't. It's quite an enjoyable taste, somewhat reminiscent of mint julip.

Israel, being only a waterway away from Italy, has also fallen victim to an espresso invasion and all the fashionable boulevards abound with locally produced chromium-plated monsters which spout tiny cups of black syrup.

Cream is rarely added to the Israeli coffee, but milk and sugar are grudgingly available.

About the closest thing to an old-fashioned American cup of

coffee with cream and sugar is something called "cafe affooch," which means "coffee upside down," or about 50-50 coffee-milk. Unless you have a cast-iron stomach, my advice is to have your first cup of coffee in Israel upside down.

NO SEGREGATION HERE

During most of my formative years in America I was always in close relationship to the American Negro. Having lived in Detroit and Cleveland, I can only draw from personal experience in these two cities, but I'm certain that one of the sociological facts of twentieth-century urban America is that old Jewish neighborhoods eventually become populated by Negroes. Many of the largest Negro churches in America were once former synagogues.

I vividly recall the old Jewish center synagogues in Cleveland: two magnificent structures, the second costing close to a million dollars, both of which were eventually sold to Negroes; and in both cases, the Star of David was left intact on the buildings. Negro churches in America probably have more interfaith symbols than any other congregations.

Perhaps in the new America that is emerging, and must emerge, from the Negroes, fight for equality, people of all races will be able to live in harmony, and black and "gilded" ghettoes will disappear. Israel is setting an example of its own. Surprisingly, to me at least, Israel has a number of indigenous Negroes in its population. Most are black Sudanese who only a generation or two were slaves for their Arab masters and have adopted their customs, religion, and dress. These people are a minute percentage of the population and do not total at the most more than a few thousand souls. They are, however, a striking people and it is an impressive sight to see a black African Bedouin family in full flowing regalia in their tents by the wayside. Let's hope the Ministry of Housing does not succeed in shikunizing this colorful people for a few generations at least.

Israel's greatest contribution to interracial harmony has been its Afro-Asian Institutes. Every year hundreds of students from new African and Asian states come to live and learn in Israel.

There has been much success and some failure. It is particularly fitting that a people that has suffered so much in the past from a hostile world should, in their rebirth, share their freedom with a people with a similar burden.

BAR MITZVAH COUNTRY STYLE

If you should get misdirected and take the train from Tel Aviv to Beersheba instead of Jerusalem—I don't know why any one else would get on a Beersheba train—you'll pass through a little train stop called Naan. This is a very lovely kibbutz whose fame is slowly spreading around the world because of the high quality lawn sprinklers manufactured there, bearing the trademark "Naan." In fact, rumor has it that these are imported into Cyprus in quantities large enough to water down any Greek-Turkish feud and then reexported to our famous cotton-growing neighbors to the south.

My most indelible impression of Naan, however, is not a wet one but a fiery one, of an evening we spent there a year ago. We had made friends with a gracious kibbutz couple and were invited to their middle son's Bar Mitzvah. Actually, we got an official invitation from the whole kibbutz, since theoretically it is a share-the-son society. The date on the invitation was May 1, which was nice, since it is an official holiday in Israel, but the day and the time were strange—Tuesday at 8:00 P.M. Having never attended a Bar Mitzvah on anything other than a Shabbat morning we figured we were in for a treat.

We arrived at the kibbutz around 6:30 and the parking lot was already jammed. Boy, we thought, this kid must have a lot of friends.

We started into the kibbutz and saw a party going on in the first row of *shikkunim* to our left that looked suspiciously like a Bar Mitzvah celebration. It wasn't our friends' home, but we figured we'd inquire. Maybe one of his kibbutz fathers was throwing a shindig. Nope, it was another boy's Bar Mitzvah; Yoram's was taking place at his real parents' home. On the way there we passed another Bar Mitzvah party and I marveled at the socialist syncopation that had produced all these male offspring at the same time.

The Bar Mitzvah reception at Yoram's was typical of any

Yiddish family gathering with all the uncles, cousins, aunts, and friends, and with none of the gaudiness that has perverted these affairs in recent years in America. We were sitting on the grass chewing the kosher fat when someone mentioned it was time to go to the amphitheater for the ceremony.

"The what?"

"The ceremony."

"What ceremony?"

"The Bar Mitzvah ceremony of course."

Well, why not? I have always been an advocate of the shul-under-the-sky theory. I figured the Lord has created some pretty nice places to pray without boxing them up, so we collected our kids and headed for the amphitheater.

What a mob. People were pouring out of all the kibbutz pathways and converging on the open area, where hundreds of bleacher-type stands had been erected.

"This Yoram must be some kid to draw a crowd like this."

"What do you mean Yoram," my knowing friend replied. "This is a Bar Mitzvah for all the kids in the kibbutz who were thirteen this year."

Wow, I thought, I wonder who has the *tallis* (prayer shawl) concession in this place. (As it turned out the poor guy would have gone broke.)

When we finally made it to the bleachers, they were pretty full up, but we managed to grab some soapbox seats in the front row.

The dirt floor of the amphitheater was dark, but there were some temporary spotlights strung out among the trees, shining on the crowd, and I estimated the attendance at three thousand people.

The lights dimmed and a voice boomed out from the loudspeakers, "The Hatikvah" — which was sung with gusto to the accompaniment of a scratching record.

The voice boomed out again, "The Internationale."

"The what!" I said, looking at my wife who was looking at me in utter amazement.

Actually, I had learned "The Internationale" in, of all places, my American high school when, in World War II days, it was part of a patriotic program to learn the national anthems of all the United Nations, including Russia. But sing it here? In Israel? I kept my mouth shut, put on my most disgusted look, and stared straight ahead.

There were quite a few nonsingers this time, including all the strained faced religious relatives of the participants who had come from all over Israel for the celebration. I was especially drawn to observe a bearded patriarch who sat in stupified awe as the ceremony progressed.

It is probably only natural for a socialist commune to sing the socialist international anthem on May Day, but still carrying a trace of Cohn and Schinecosis in my unconscious, the spectacle was a shock to me.

As "The Internationale" died away new scratchy martial music flared up and about forty of the healthiest, toughest-looking thirteen-year-olds I have ever seen marched onto the field carrying kerosene soaked torches.

There was the customary welcoming speech from the Movement elder with the Ben Gurion-like brow, the handshaking, more martial music, and then some more speeches as the Bar Mitzvah kids gazed apprehensively at their slowly extinguishing torches. Finally the actual Bar Mitzvah began. Three or four kids broke from the ranks and dashed helter-skelter to some large poles in the background. A quick application of the torch and whoosh, five fiery pillars zoomed heavenward.

What happened next is difficult to describe, since unless you were trained at Barnum and Bailey, you couldn't take it all in at once. Kids leaped over obstacles, kids climbed trees, kids swung by ropes, kids leaped over each other's shoulders; in short a fantastic, fiery gymnastic phantasmagoria that grew in crescendo until the final test of courage—a parachute jump sans parachute.

In the rear center of the area was a log and rope construction about forty feet high. The Bar Mitzvah kids climbed to the top in groups of seven or eight. When they reached the rickety top, they held a piece of bent wire over their heads, centered it on a guide wire, and jumped off into space, descending to the ground at about a fifty degree angle.

I could just picture American mothers letting their kids jump off a tower like that. Any self-respecting Jewish mother wouldn't even let the kid climb past the fifth rung.

The kids were superb. If anyone was terrified, it was the uninitiated, like us, among the audience.

After this climactic spectacle, an arch of kerosene soaked rags was lit in front of the stands, and, as their names were called, the kids leaped through the flames to receive their singed Bar Mitzvah certificates.

God wasn't mentioned once during the proceedings, but He must have been awful busy that night watching over those kids.

WON'T WE EVER LEARN?

Somewhere in this saga is the sad tale of my archeological ineptness, the digging up of half the homestead without acquiring any Leviticus scrolls. Eventually, however, I was successful, thanks to the unwelcome assistance of one G. A. Nasser.

It began a week before the war. Or was it two? Those days of awe and glory are sharply chiseled in every Israeli's mind, but the weeks of tension before the war, when the country and everyone in it was a coiled spring, are still jumbled and hazy. Anyway, it was the week of the decision to dig.

For days the community was rife with rumors. *We're supposed to dig trenches—don't dig trenches, you'll alarm the children—do dig trenches, be prepared.* Finally I began to dig when I heard from my friend who was a bosom buddy of the area civil defense chief that orders were going to be given the next day to dig. They weren't, so it turned out that I was about two days ahead of most people, which may have been a physical advantage but certainly not a psychological one.

One of the frustrations of being an American in Israel in time of war is the feeling that you're somewhat useless because you're not liable for military service. At least I did not have a mundane civilian occupation and was working eleven hours a day in an aircraft factory, but the night hours hung like an anvil and I welcomed the chance to dig.

The first night was a complete washout. I got down about a foot, which didn't provide enough shelter for our cat, who contrary to the popular saying, was probably the only unscared member of our household.

The next night, I hit clay dirt. I had strung up a light so that I could work at night and developed a John Henry-like rhythmical swing, which whacked away at the clay. My cat would feel pretty safe that night.

By the third day, things began to shape up and I had a pretty impressive slit trench about hip deep in my back yard.

The parallel to grave digging was almost a constant companion. A phrase from the Rosh Hashanah service, which I had passed over unnoticed until that particular New Year, kept revolving in my mind: "And of the inhabitants of the Sharon he prayed that their homes shall not be their graves." The English is cold and sterile, but the Hebrew, "*shebatayhem lo yehye kvarahem*," has a marvelous hypnotic rhythm to it. For that reason I put a 30 degree angle in the trench, which gave it a decided military look.

Halfway through the trench, I received a great deal of encouragement and occasional assistance from David, Elana, and Elissa, who hauled dirt and conducted tours for the neighborhood children.

About four feet down I began to hit, what in my non-agricultural mind I assume is, virgin soil: red-brown, uniform, no plants, no roots, no organic matter, just soil. Another foot and the soil began to get softer; then at five-and-one-half feet I found the only stone I had come across in the entire excavation process. It was a rock chipped like a spearhead and next to it was some cord matter and the remains of a possible shaft. In my amateur archeological eyes, it certainly was a genuine enough spearhead, perhaps 10,000 to 20,000 years old.

I ran to show my delightful find to my wife. She looked at it with her profound womanly wisdom and said, "Twenty-thousand years. Won't man ever learn?"

VOLUNTEERS

I got the call about an hour before Shabbat. "Look, this is Eli from the Association of Americans and Canadians in Israel. Got about seventy volunteers flying in tonight and some of them are religious and don't want to travel on the Sabbath. Can you put them up for the weekend?"

If nothing else our community is overorganized and oozes with spirit, so I figured I'd have no problem accommodating them even on such short notice.

"How many?" I asked.

"About three or four."

"OK, no problem."

I telephoned neighbors and arrangements were made. Then the phone rang.

"Hello, this is Eli again, er . . . how about fifteen?"

"Fifteen? OK."

Why not? We could probably use as many of these kids as we can get. More phone calls, more arrangements, and the Shabbat twilight began to descend. Another phone call.

"Hello, this is Eli again, there a . . . , there a . . . there may be as many as forty."

"Are you sure you're not Abraham trying to save Sodom?" I asked.

"Look, I'm sorry, we just don't know. We don't have any passenger manifests and we couldn't tell anyway who is religious."

"OK, we'll do our best."

As our religious community prepared for a siege, they descended upon us, not forty, not fifteen, but just five wonderful young people.

The first boy up the walk was a roly-poly rabbinical student carrying a guitar. All his other luggage had been lost, but his precious guitar was still with him. It was still about a half hour until sundown, so he sat down and played us a lovely psalm. It turned out that he was a semi-pro, having been an accompanist to an American Jewish folk singer known as the Singing Rabbi. The three other boys were a jeweler from London, a professor from Boston University, and another student from the Jewish Theological Seminary.

The girl had an excellent job in the State Department and had given it up to fly here in these crucial days. She had a sister who lived in a religious *moshav* and she wanted to be with her. The sister, incidentally, thought the girl was completely out of her mind when she arrived at her home.

They were received graciously and with open arms by the local citizenry and spent their first Shabbat in Israel in the tranquility of our quiet town. That night I drove them into Tel Aviv, which was going full blast at a tremendous tempo. There were a few sandbags around and a few more than usual soldiers in combat gear, but the only real signs of abnormality were the practically empty Dan Hotel, and the abuse which a passerby heaped on a corner beatnick who was playing a guitar and singing, his hat on the sidewalk for donations: "Coward, why aren't you on the border with the rest of the youth?"

Next morning, Sunday, four of the boys left for their destination, kibbutz Lavi in the Galilee, and the girl left for her sister's. As the professor was also a scientist and I felt it was a shame for him to flick chickens at such a crucial time, he stayed around another day while I tried to put him in touch with people who might be interested in his experience. But he still craved his kibbutz, so Monday morning we drove him to the Geha road junction near Tel Aviv, and he got out to hitchhike his way to kibbutz Chafetz Chaim in the south. It was about 8:00 A.M. The war started at 8:30.

STARS OF A SUMMER NIGHT, 1967

The twentieth-century American civilian is a fortunate creature: he has never been bombed or, if we discount any localized World War II exercises, experienced a total blackout. There is nothing so ugly as a bombing, but there was a spectacular, awesome beauty that preceded my first, and hopefully last, bombing in Israel.

Dusk descends quickly in Israel, but on that Monday night in June it seemed to hesitate and quiver as if in fear of what the night would bring. It would be poetic to say that the lights went out one by one, but they did not. Instead, they did not go on.

The last rays of sunlight filtered through the dust and nowhere was a light lit to penetrate the enveloping gloom. It was as if God had built a heavenly planetarium over Israel and hung out each star from the roof. I had never seen its equal. If Bible scholars seek a reason for the prevalence of prophecy in ancient Israel, let them spend a night in the open under such a sky.

I think the glory of it must have struck at Jordanian hearts, too, because there was a pause—a short one, but a pause—before the entire night sky opened up into a cacophony of hell.

The guns became silent at about four o'clock, but by then the dawn was beginning to creep in over the mountains of Judea and the inky blackness was subdued.

This was a night to remember. I pray that it may ever be a memory and never again a reality.

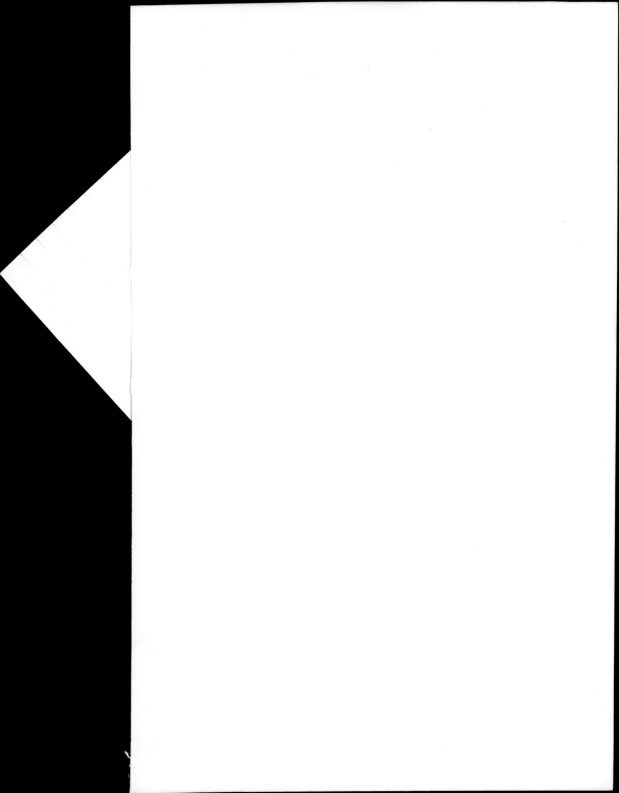

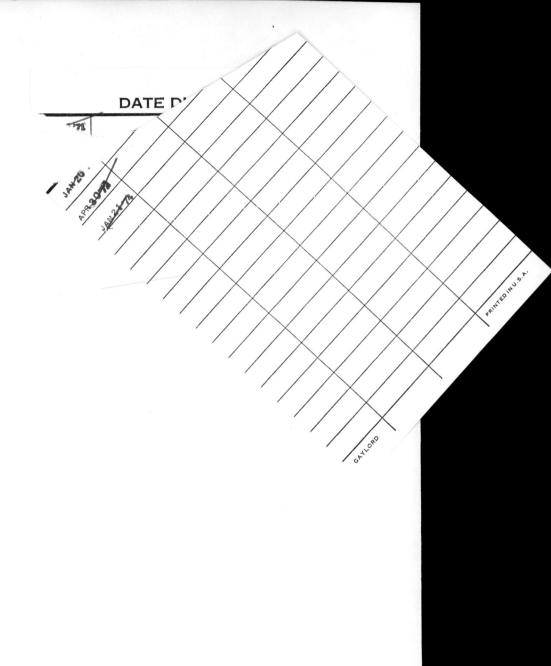

DATE D

JAN 20

APR 30

JAN 24

PRINTED IN U.S.A.

GAYLORD